OLD TITLE DEEDS
A Guide for Local and Family Historians

OLD TITLE DEEDS
A Guide for Local and Family Historians

N.W. Alcock

Phillimore

2001

First published in 1986

Second Edition published by
PHILLIMORE & CO. LTD.
Shopwyke Manor Barn, Chichester, West Sussex

ISBN 1 86077 160 2

Printed and bound in Great Britain by
BIDDLES LTD.
Guildford, Surrey

To M.A., C.G., D.L., L.L., G.O'S., S.T.,
and their colleagues
whose care gave a flying start to this book.

Contents

LIST OF ILLUSTRATIONS

LIST OF TABLES

ABBREVIATIONS

PRO   Public Record Office.
SBT   Shakespeare Birthplace Trust Record Office, Stratford-upon-Avon, Warwickshire.
WRO Warwickshire County Record Office, Warwick.

ACKNOWLEDGEMENTS

This book has been built on uncountable hours spent in record offices, where I have received never-failing assistance from the staff. They are far too numerous to name individually, but I hope they will accept my thanks collectively. M.W. Farr, M. Ory, C.J. Arnison, R. Chamberlain–Brothers, and R.A. Storey were kind enough to read the text in draft. They made many helpful comments and corrections, but do not necessarily share the views expressed. The first-named also kindly checked the transcripts of medieval texts. J.B. Post advised on the deed resources of the Public Record Office. Permission to reproduce the deeds used in the illustrations has kindly been given by the following: Messrs. Heath and Blenkinsop (Illus.14, 15, 19, 20); Mr. G. Holbech (Illus.2, 17, 21); Sir Robert Throckmorton (Illus.24); the Trustees of Holy Trinity Church Estate, Coventry (Illus.1); the Shakespeare Birthplace Trust (Illus. 28(b)); Warwickshire County Record Office (Illus.22, 23, 25, 26); Yorkshire Archaeological Society (Illus.28(a)). Additional information and comments will be gratefully received for incorporation in any future edition.

N.W. ALCOCK
Leamington Spa

Preface to Second Edition

In the 15 years since *Old Title Deeds* first appeared, the enthusiastic responses of readers have assured me that the book is achieving its aim of making deeds more accessible as history. In preparing this new edition, I have been able to incorporate a wide variety of corrections and suggestions from both experts in the field and ordinary readers for which I am most grateful. As well as a general updating of information and the addition of references to recent publications, two sections have been extensively revised.

The first is that on using computers for studying deeds. Computer technology has changed almost out of all recognition in the last decade, as has the availability of digital resources to the individual user. At home or in the record office, they can now call on facilities that were previously only available from a large main-frame computer. The second major revision enlarges the discussion of manorial documents and copies of court roll into a separate section of Chapter 4. Several handbooks and guides to the use of manorial records have been produced, but none cover their recording of property transactions in any detail. I have myself recently used manor court rolls for tracing families and their property, and have come to appreciate how valuable a good run of court rolls is for this purpose.

Accessibility and indexing of major deed collections, such as those of the Public Record Office, continues to improve, so that further updating will undoubtedly become necessary. Any additional corrections or comments for future revision will be gratefully received.

N.W. Alcock
Leamington Spa

1

INTRODUCTION

Deeds can be the ugly ducklings of the record office, bedraggled, dirty and ignored, but it is the purpose of this book to show how they may be used to create, if not a fleet of swans, then at least a well-constructed historical study. They are by far the most numerous but the least used source of historical evidence, surviving in their thousands in collection after collection in record offices, libraries, and muniment rooms up and down the country, and even overseas. Their neglect has been partly because they can be difficult to understand, written in technical language and often in Latin. It is also because the information they contain can be summarised in a few lines, and therefore seems insignificant. This ignores the possibility of writing the history of a community by correlating the evidence of a group of deeds. For family history in particular, they are an almost totally neglected resource, even though one single deed may supply crucial links in a sequence of family relationships.

The book is primarily intended for people without extensive historical training, and therefore concentrates especially on the two branches of history where 'amateurs' most often begin their historical research—local history and family history. Of course, people with a great deal of skill are also working in these areas, and they have probably learnt most of the information presented here in the same way as the author, simply by working with deeds. I hope that they and other 'professionals' may find something interesting as well.

The scope of the book is defined by the three questions it sets out to answer: Why should local and family historians use deeds, and what sort of historical information can they expect and hope to obtain? Where should they look for deeds and what should the deeds concern? How can their evidence be extracted? The last is the most important question, and occupies the largest of the three main chapters of the book. It examines post-medieval deeds first because these are easier to decipher than the medieval ones covered in the second section. In each the different types of deeds likely to be encountered are analysed clause by clause, to show how the parts containing important information can be separated from the legal jargon and repetition. The technical problems, such as methods of dating, that may perplex the less experienced are also covered. This chapter is essentially practical rather than theoretical, and avoids exhaustive legal detail.

The second chapter is intended as a guide to locating deeds relating to particular people and places. In this task, initial failure may well *not* mean that the evidence does not exist, because local deeds can be scattered throughout the country, and even abroad. This chapter also looks at the clues that a bundle of deeds itself may give, and how these may help in the discovery of related evidence.

The first chapter tries to remedy the neglect of deeds by historians, by demonstrating some of their uses. It reviews the information that can be found in deeds, and how they illuminate historical evidence for a wide range of topics divided broadly into the history of places and things, and the history, of people and families. It also includes a discussion of the application of computers to the study of deeds. The balance between what computers can achieve, as against the difficulty and effort needed, is crucial in assessing their usefulness.

Appendices include the texts of typical deeds, provide a suitable form for recording and abstracting deeds, and illustrate post-medieval letter forms. Suggestions for further reading are also given, and a glossary includes brief explanations of the principal terms relating to deeds.

The book deals specifically with English and Welsh deeds, which are identical in form. Deeds relating to Ireland follow the same patterns, with occasional idiosyncrasies in wording or layout. In Scotland, however, land tenure depended on Roman law, and title deeds show completely different form which are beyond the scope of this book.[1] It will be observed that the great majority of the examples relate to the Midlands, especially Warwickshire, and in particular almost all the urban ones are drawn from Coventry. The deeds from one area are virtually identical to those from any other, and so I have chosen examples from those within my own knowledge, rather than searching for them elsewhere. The Coventry deeds have been encountered in the course of a detailed study of the city that has been in progress for a number of years. As this city combines great medieval prosperity, 18th-century growth, and 19th-century industrialisation, with excellent survival of deeds from the 12th century onwards, their evidence as a whole probably exceeds that from most cities; of course, other places provide their own particular insights.[2]

The only previous aids for historians working with deeds are the short books by J. Cornwall and A.A. Dibben (see Further Reading). Both are useful, but their scale prevents them from including more than the most straightforward analysis. A couple of articles in local publications are also often referred to (by A.G. Foster and R.B. Pugh); both these are helpful in explaining conveyancing practice, but go no further. Textbooks by eminent lawyers describe the land law through the centuries. It is amazingly difficult to match the content of a specific deed with their descriptions of its function, and such prominent features as the dower trustee (see p.63) find no mention in their pages. The most useful guide might be one of the many 18th-century text books on conveyancing (e.g. Gilbert Horsman, *Precedents in Conveyancing*, 3rd ed., 1768) or an attorney's *vade-mecum* of the 18th or 19th centuries, such as F.C. Jones, *Attorney's Pocketbook* (1841), but readers are unlikely to have easy access to these. I hope the present book will help to fill the gap between all these.

---

[1] No simple guide to Scottish deeds has been produced, but a useful introduction is given by R.F. Dell, 'Some differences between Scottish and English Archives', *J. Society of Archivists*, 3 (1968), pp. 386-397. The most significant aspect as far as property is concerned is that systematic registration of sales began as early as the 16th century and is generally complete from the 17th century onwards.

[2] For example, 17th-century industrial housing is not significant in Coventry, but deed evidence has been effectively used in Frome, Somerset: see R. Leech, *Early Industrial Housing: The Trinity Area of Frome*, H.M.S.O., 1981.

1 Lease of a Coventry house for ten years from 24 June 1223. This is one of the earliest known deeds for a small property that includes a date, at least by implication. Because the lease was for a specified period, it had to state exactly when it started: the feast of the Birth of St John the Baptist, the third after the Translation of St Thomas Martyr (i.e. St Thomas à Becket who was translated on 7 July 1220). Deeds at this social level were not routinely dated until almost a century later, and the unusual way the date is specified shows that the standard procedure had not yet evolved. For text see p.103. [WRO DR564/205]

One aspect of old deeds that can be overlooked in their detailed examination is their fascination as historical objects, beyond their significance as historical evidence. The only way most of us will see a 12th- or 13th-century manuscript outside a showcase is in the form of a deed (Illus.1), while the historian's eye should not necessarily glaze over even when faced by a pile of post-medieval deeds. Take, for example, an 18th-century deed in Warwick Record Office. When opened (Illus.2), it contained a complete series of small deeds as clean and perfect as the day they were written. They started with the original grant in 1505 of an annuity (annual payment) by the owner of the manor of Burton Dassett, Warwickshire, which was transferred from family to family until all the deeds were folded up together in 1757. Although the record office staff had examined them, they had left them in the original arrangement (see p.52), so that we can handle the same prized and valuable possession as did the members of the Makepeace and Neale families.

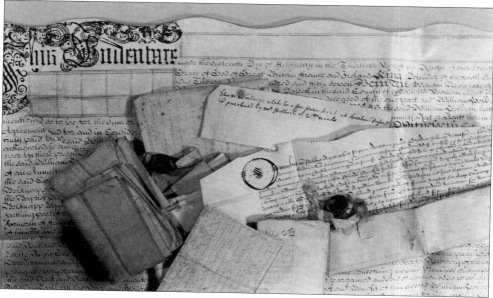

2   Deed of 1757, transferring an annuity of 24s 6d, payable from the manor of Burton Dassett, Warwickshire, with the earlier deeds for the annuity back to its original grant in 1505. These were found folded into the 1757 deed. [WRO CR457/Box 5, Loose B]

3   Wooden deed boxes dating from the 16th to the 18th century (judging from the writing of the contemporary labels). They were made to hold the deeds for the lands with which Lapwroth church, Warwickshire, was endowed. A deed box of this type was known as a ' skippet', and the term is also applied to the tin boxes used to hold the seals of Recoveries. [WRO DR(B) 35]

4   Family settlement (Release of Lease and Release, containing 80 membranes) of 1802 for the Seymour family of Ragley Hall, Warwickshire (the family of the Marquis of Hertford). The release of a large family settlement needs considerable athleticism and great patience to disentangle, but can be expected to contain detailed descriptions of vast estates and the names of numerous relatives. [WRO CR114A/9]

Occasionally special containers, usually wooden boxes, were made for deeds (Illus.3). To visit a farm, be shown the 17th-century deed box, and open it to find the deeds still inside, as I have done once, is truly to touch history (despite the feeling that the deeds might be safer in the record office). Even the driest of 18th-century family settlements (Illus.4) evokes images of Georgian mansions surrounded by parkland and tenant farms, all of which are described in the deed; its record of the squire, his wife and children, parallels the Gainsboroughs in his hall.

2

WHY?

The two main sections of this chapter are divided according to subject. The first involves the use of deeds as evidence for places and for things, which are particularly the concern of the local historian, and the second their evidence for people, linked rather more to the family historian. However, the applications of deeds, and their relevance to different types of history inevitably overlap from one section to the other. The third part examines the use of computers to analyse deeds and their historical evidence. Some technicalities are mentioned, but the main concern is with the advantages—what can be discovered using computers that would be difficult or impossible without them—and the problems.

DEEDS FOR PLACES AND FOR THINGS

THE LAND

By their nature, deeds are a fundamental source for the history of the land. Documents such as Land Tax lists and church or poor rates identify the land-owners by name, but only deeds show precisely what their property consisted of in land, buildings, and other rights, who was the real owner of a given property, and whether it was freehold, copyhold, held on a three-life lease, part of a marriage settlement, or mortgaged to the last blade of grass. For agrarian history, deeds can be used to reconstruct the patterns of farms and their fields and to follow their development by working back from the earliest available detailed map. Changes in farm size relate directly to the social structure of a community, and to the balance between wealth and poverty. Alterations in fields can be evidence for changing patterns of husbandry, such as a conversion from arable to stock farming. Deeds also give direct evidence for this and other aspects of agricultural practice, such as the draining or cultivation of marshes and moors.[1]

Understanding and mapping enclosed fields is easy compared to dealing with an open-field system, the most complex element in the agrarian landscape. Most deeds only describe open-field farms in outline, listing the number of yardlands

---

[1] C. Clay's survey, 'Landlords and Estate Management in England' (in J. Thirsk (ed.) *Agrarian History of England: vol. V, 1640-1750*, Cambridge University Press, 1985, vol.ii, p.119) builds on a very wide range of evidence, principally from deeds, to draw a comprehensive picture of the development of estates and the correlation between types of tenure and farming practice in the 17th and 18th centuries. For map reconstruction, see for example N.W. Alcock, 'Fields and Farms in an East Devon Parish', *Report and Transactions of the Devonshire Association* (hereafter *Trans Devonshire Assoc.*), 107 (1975), p.93.

or virgates (standard units of land measurement, nominally representing 32 acres, though their actual size varied considerably from place to place). These deeds therefore illustrate the regularity (or usually the reverse) of the division of the open fields between different properties. Occasionally, deeds include a list of the component strips of the holding, generally with the names of the owners of adjoining strips (the abuttals) (Illus.18). The mass of information this gives about the open-field system, with the names of fields and furlongs, and the distribution of strips amongst them, throws light on cultivation systems and the organisation of holdings. The abuttals should name a large number of villagers, but if most strips have the same neighbours, this is a strong indication of a regular strip layout, perhaps of the 'solskifte' or 'sun-sequence' type (in which the sequence of owners of strips repeated that of the houses in the village street); this has been found in some northern villages.[2] Post-medieval deeds, and especially leases, also illuminate agriculture practice in other ways, including requirements to spread manure, or to pay extra rent if more than a certain area is ploughed. Both these and medieval leases may also demand special rents, e.g. in corn, fish, or poultry, or in special services, such as help with the harvest, or the carriage of stone, coal, or crops.

A notable example of the application of deed evidence to rural history is the study by W.G. Hoskins of Wigston Magna, Leicestershire (*The Midland Peasant*, Leicester University Press, 1961) which uses the deeds relating to the endowment of a 16th-century hospital as its principal medieval source.

LAND OWNERSHIP

The purchasers and vendors, landlords and tenants, named in a series of deeds reveal the nature of local land-ownership, whether it was widely dispersed or concentrated in a few hands, and how this changed with time. They also show the social status of the property owners, and whether they were local people or outsiders looking for an investment. For urban property, the relationship between town and country is particularly significant. Did rural landowners buy urban property and vice-versa, or did the two lead separate lives? As an illustration, in the 17th and 18th centuries, it was not uncommon for Coventrians to buy farms in nearby villages; sometimes this was for very practical reasons, as shown by a lease of 1629 for a farm three miles away, which reserved the right for the owner to use the house 'at all such time as there shall be any infection of the plague in Coventry.'[3] The reverse, of country people owning Coventry property, was almost unknown, apart from the successful townsfolk who retired to the country; even these tended to sell their town property quite soon. Hugh Capell, mercer (mayor of Coventry in 1698) moved to Sutton-under-Brailes in south Warwickshire, where he died in 1704. His daughter disposed of his Coventry house and shop in 1739.

---

[2] See under *sun-division* in A.R.H. Baker and R.A. Butlin (eds.), *Studies of Field Systems in the British Isles* (Cambridge University Press, 1973).

[3] Coventry Record Office, Miscellaneous Deeds box 33.

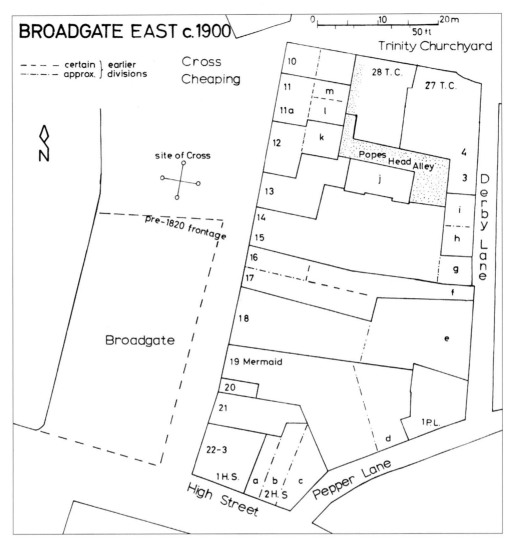

5 Nineteenth-century property boundaries for a part of central Coventry. Dashed lines show alterations recorded in Deeds. Illus.5 and 6 are from N.W. Alcock, 'Documentary Records', in Margaret Rylatt and Michael A. Stokes, *The Excavations at Broadgate East, Coventry 1974-5.*

TOWNS

Deeds illustrate urban history in a wide variety of ways, from street and house layouts, to building dates and financial arrangements.[4] For topographical evidence, urban deeds are even more valuable than rural ones, because the unit of property

[4] For a survey see D. Keene, 'The Medieval Urban Environment in Documentary Records', *Archives*, 16 (1983), pp. 137-44. An excellent short explanation of the use of deeds to study urban topography in Nottingham is given by S. Mastoris, *History in the Making* (City of Nottingham Museums, 1985), p. 11. An interesting case study by the same author using deed evidence back to the mid-14th century is in S.P. Douglass, A.G. MacCormick and S.N. Mastoris, 'The old 'Flying Horse', Nottingham: a structural and documentary survey', *Trans Thoroton Soc.*, 91 (1987), pp.115-25.

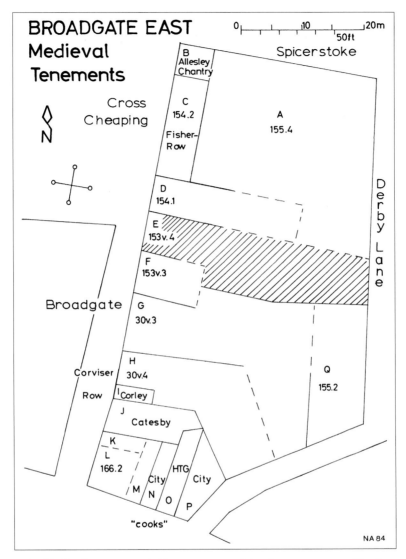

6 Medieval tenements (with some owners) in the same area as illus.5, based on the evidence of Coventry Priory cartulary (references 154.2, etc.) and of 53 original deeds. The Priory owned the shaded tenement, but collected rents from eight others. HTG stands for the Guild of the Holy Trinity, which was a major property owner in the city. The remarkably irregular pattern probably arose from the sub-division of one or two large properties.

(the single house site or tenement) is much smaller than a farm, and needs more precise identification, akin to that for an individual open-field strip; the deed normally names the street and the abuttals (the adjacent owners). In the 19th century, large-scale plans of individual tenements were often drawn on deeds, and can be used to reconstruct the overall tenement layout for part or all of a town. Illustration 5 shows an example of this for a small area in central Coventry. Urban boundaries were often extremely stable, so that the early layout may be worked out by combining later plans with the evidence of a series of deeds running back into the medieval period. This has been achieved for a few places, e.g. Oxford,[5] and should be possible for many more. Illustration 6 shows the same area as illustration 5 in the medieval period, revealing, for example, two rows of shops for specialist trades, the fishmongers and the shoemakers (corvisers) which disappeared in the 17th century.

Such plans, and the precise location of the property described in particular deeds, throw light on the town's topographical development, and on the social character of its different parts.[6] The location of occupiers, whether owners or tenants, is also very useful in relation to other evidence, particularly probate records. For example, it allows probate inventories to be linked to standing buildings, and the correlation of prosperity with locality.

FINANCE

The economic implications of deeds are sometimes concealed, with no better information given than that a sale was 'for good consideration'. However, after about 1600 the money involved is usually stated explicitly, and changes in value can be followed. This naturally has to be done with care, taking account of such factors as alterations in the precise size of the property. It is also important to make certain that the figure cited is the full value, not reduced by a mortgage (and indeed that the deed records a sale and not a mortgage). In towns, where the value of the buildings makes up a higher proportion of the total then for most rural property, their state of repair was obviously very important in setting the price. This cannot usually be discovered directly, though deeds may note that the premises or part of them were 'in decay' or 'ruinous'. The prices themselves sometimes suggest this by showing a sudden increase when other property values remain constant, implying a substantial addition or a rebuilding.

The results of these comparisons can be surprising. Thus, two houses built in the elegant Clarendon Crescent in Leamington Spa, Warwickshire in 1832-4 cost £1,150 and £1,350. Thereafter, their value declined steadily, reaching a low point in 1898 (£550 and £405 respectively). Only in the 1950s did they again fetch as much as when they were built. The expectation that house values always increase was no more valid in the 1850s than in the 1980s.

Another aspect of finance in relation to property is its use as security for loans. From the 17th century onwards, lawyers developed forms of mortgage deed that were relatively safe, both for the lender (mortgagee), that he would

5   H.E. Salter, *Map of Medieval Oxford* (Oxford University Press, 1934).
6   An excellent example on a very small scale is M. Prior, *Fisher Row: Fishermen, Bargemen and Canal Boatmen in Oxford: 1500-1900* (Clarendon Press, 1982).

recover his money, and for the borrower (mortgagor), that he would not be unjustly dispossessed. These deeds are very numerous among title deeds. Not only were many purchases followed by mortgages, but frequently while a mortgage continued, it would be transferred from one lender to another.

Before about 1600, mortgages had a very different character. Receiving interest for a loan was prohibited as 'usury' until 1571, and instead the lender would take possession of the property and collect the rents, etc. Furthermore, failure to repay the loan by the specified date led to the permanent forfeiture of the property,[7] though in practice, this danger might be reduced by choosing a friend or relative as mortgagee. Curiously, the use of mortgages in the 16th century seems to have been very irregular. Thus in Devon they were not uncommon, but in the Midlands they seem to be very rare.[8] In contrast, a sample of late 16th-century wills from Wales contain numerous references to mortgages that were unlikely to be redeemed.[9]

Through the 17th and 18th centuries, when a single house or small farm was involved, mortgagees can be expected to be local people: well-to-do yeoman farmers, and particularly in towns local craftsmen (including in 18th-century Coventry, bakers, hatters, weavers, and smiths); widows were also prominent, probably because they had money at their disposal, left them by their husbands. The mortgagees lending large sums on the security of big landed estates often seem to have been Londoners, but have no other obvious factors in common.

The pattern began to change by the beginning of the 19th century in towns at least, with the involvement of more people of what might be described as professional classes—attorneys (solicitors), bankers (first as individuals and then representing their banks), and those simply described as 'gentlemen' or 'esquire' (i.e. people of some status though not necessarily of independent means). Later in the century, building societies began to take a part. They had their roots in true 'building' associations, putting up houses for their members. These started on a small and informal scale like the 'Hare and Squirrel' Coventry Union Building Society, founded in 1821 and meeting monthly in the public house of that name. They later extended their activities to lending on the security of existing houses. The timescale of these changes probably varied very much from community to community, if indeed the pattern was the same everywhere. It has been found that the 19th-century development of the London suburbs was substantially financed from investment by the trustees of family and marriage settlements;[10] preliminary work on provincial towns suggests that such investment was much less important outside the capital.

---

[7] Technically, there was no equity of redemption, by which the mortgagor could exercise a right to redeem his land, even though he had failed to pay his debt in time. For a discussion of the development of this concept, see D. Sugarman and R Warrington, 'Land law, citizenship, and the invention of "Englishness": The strange world of the equity of redemption', in J. Brewer and S. Staves (eds.), *Early Modern Concepts of Property* (Routledge, 1995), pp. 111-144

[8] See J.E. Kew, 'Mortgages in Mid-Tudor Devonshire', *Trans Devonshire Ass.*, 99 (1967), p.165. In the Midlands, references to mortgages in either deeds or wills seem to be almost non-existent at this period.

[9] See for example National Library of Wales, Brecon Probate Copy Register I, p.467 (Thomas ap Kydwgan, 1578); II, p. 629 (Hugh Price, 1588).

[10] H. Dyos, *Exploring the Urban Past* (Cambridge University Press, 1982), p.171.

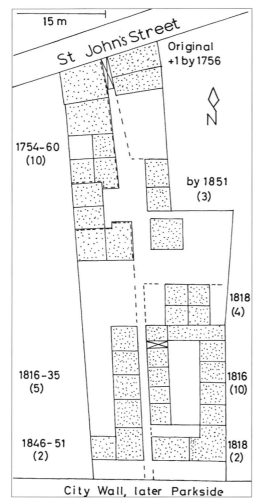

7 The development of a Coventry court: 46-7 St John's Street, mainly based on the evidence of one document, an abstract of title of 1818. In 1754, the property consisted of a house facing St John's Street, with a garden and orchard behind, stretching back to the city wall; the north-east corner of the original plot had been cut off at some much earlier date. Between 1754 and 1760 ten new houses were erected along the west side of the property. After this came a pause until 1816, when the plot was sold off in five separate parts; the whole court was then filled in until, by 1851, it contained at least 37 houses, including four facing the new street, Parkside, on the line of the city wall. [Coventry City Council, Deed Bundle 1330; Coventry R. O. 491/14/1]

BUILDINGS

The age of houses is often of special interest to local historians. Deeds may give excellent dating evidence, but this cannot be guaranteed, and the chances of success depend very much on the type of house and its location, and on the period concerned. Information about buildings in deeds earlier than 1600 is very rare, and the correlation of surviving buildings with the early deeds for them is also difficult. Unfortunately, this excludes many of the houses that are hardest to date in other ways. For medieval manor houses or those of similar status, it is often supposed that a house is more likely to be rebuilt after a change of ownership than at another time, and deed evidence can be used to give more precision to an approximate architectural date. The argument is obviously not a strong one!

Deeds for a house built on a fresh site, or by converting farm buildings, are often more informative. If they can be followed back, the earliest ones should describe a field or barn, while the next refers to a messuage (i.e. a house). The deeds often add the name of the builder, to help confirm the legal identity of the earlier and later descriptions. A particularly interesting deed from Stoneleigh, Warwickshire provides a rare example of a medieval building date. On 10 September 1490, the rector of the next village granted to the Abbey of Stoneleigh a new-built house of two bays and a fulling mill on a plot of land, so that its rent could pay for memorial services.[11] The plot was called 'Robcroft', and it can be identified from later documents; as it lies well away from the

---

[11] Shakespeare Birthplace Trust Record Office, DR10/996.

rest of the village, the late medieval two-bay house that still stands there is clearly the one built by the rector.

Eighteenth- and 19th-century deeds for houses in towns are much more likely to include either descriptions of buildings or information about rebuilding (statements like 'new-built in brick by ...'), presumably because the structures made up a major part of the value; care is needed, however, as 'new-built' can continue to be used for a century or more in successive documents. Periods when building work was most frequent suggest times of local prosperity.[12] Deeds (and leases in particular) may include schedules of fixtures in rooms, covering such things as doors, shelves, brewing vats, and window glass. In one Coventry house the windows of the best chamber contained '21 panes of wrought (*stained*) glass with the months of the year'. A deed of 1660 for a mercer's house and shop lists the shop fittings in detail, complementing the descriptions of contents found in probate inventories.[13]

In many towns, population pressure was relieved by converting yards and gardens into houses. Deeds are very revealing for this process, one series of mortgages revealing, for example, 'a messuage now converted into two tenements', '... with three houses behind, new-built by ...', '... now containing twelve tenements' (Illus.7). In Coventry, they reveal that this infilling was predominantly a response to population growth in the 18th rather than the 19th century.

DEVELOPMENT: HOUSES AND INDUSTRY

The outward growth of towns over green fields has been going on since at least the 17th century, and deeds give excellent evidence for it. Broadly speaking, two procedures were followed. The land-owner might grant leases (e.g. for 99 years), with a requirement for the tenant to build a house within a certain time, to certain specifications, or even to a set design. Here the archives of the landowner should be informative, and a proportion of the leases can also be expected to exist. Other property was developed as freeholdings. A field was divided into house sites which were sold individually. Each purchaser received an identical 'abstract of title' (a summary of previous ownership, see p.57), and these duplicates give an excellent chance for one or more to survive. They reveal the history of the land for up to a hundred years before the final subivision, as well as indicating the probable building date. Succeeding deeds illuminate the social character of the purchasers and their successors, as well as prices and their changes. The invisible control that was exercised by the pattern of land-ownership can often be seen in maps, and may be explained by the deed evidence.

In Leeds, for example, M.W. Beresford has examined 19th-century back-to-back housing. He has shown how curiosities of the plan, such as odd half-rows, changes in orientation, etc. relate precisely to the ownership of the underlying fields.[14] My

---

[12] See F. Sheppard, V. Belcher and P. Cottrell, 'The Middlesex and Yorkshire deeds registries and the study of building fluctuations', *London Journal*, vol.5(2) (1979), pp.176-217.

[13] Both these examples are included in N.W. Alcock, 'Documentary Records', in Margaret Rylatt and Michael A. Stokes, *The Excavations at Broadgate East, Coventry 1974-5*.

[14] M.W. Beresford, *Time and Place* (Hambledon Press, 1984), especially pp.308-94.

own house in Leamington Spa, Warwickshire, reveals one way in which such developments were financed. It was built on land belonging to the manor, and so its title deeds refer back to the sale by Queen Elizabeth in 1596. This particular field was acquired by an entrepreneur, Stephen Peasnall, in 1824 and his various mortgages are described. The actual builder, John Knibb, worked in quite a small way, and he never purchased the plot outright. Instead, he agreed with Peasnall to buy the plot at some time in the future (for £151). In 1830, he built the house, and Peasnall sold house and land for £570 (a price not exceeded until the 1950s!); Knibb received £419. The purchaser was an elderly spinster of independent means, typical of the inhabitants of the spa, who lived in the house until her death in 1854. Knibb also built the adjoining five houses, working out from the town centre, and by 1830 the inner three had been completed and were in private hands, but Peasnall still owned the remaining plots.[15]

Another example concerns Chapel Street in Warwick, lying just outside the town wall, behind the houses lining the main street. Title deeds for a number of Chapel Street houses are in Warwick Record Office, and one includes the vital abstract of title.[16] This follows the ownership of a one-acre field from 1723 when it was part of a local estate, through various sales and mortgages to 1797, when a cotton weaving factory was built on part of it. The factory only prospered briefly, because in 1819 the site was sold and laid out for housing (and each of the purchasers received his copy of the abstract).

Industrial development in the 19th century can be clearly illustrated from deeds. Factories frequently changed owners and tenants with the swings of industrial prosperity and depression, and mortgages were needed to raise working capital. Deed bundles may include documents relating to the general organisation and finance of the concern, such as partnership agreements and dissolutions, and debenture deeds (which guarantee the repayment of a loan to the company as a first charge on its assets). Occasionally schedules of debts are given following a bankruptcy, or when a mortgage or sale took place for the benefit of creditors.

Buildings made up a major part of the value of an industrial site, and the deeds often include detailed descriptions of the factory. Large-scale plans are not uncommon, and one can find two or three successive plans for the same factory as it changed owners and uses (Illus.8). Schedules of machinery and fittings may also be recorded.

DEEDS FOR PEOPLE

The simplest task for the family historian is to establish relationships—to link one person to another as father/son, husband/wife, etc. This information is also of value to the local historian in working out the social network in the community, the descent and succession of property, and the strength of links to neighbouring or

---

[15] Warwick Record Office, CR2155.
[16] See N.W. Alcock, 'The building of Chapel Street' in Nat Alcock (ed.), *The Past in Warwick: Tudors to Victorians* (University of Warwick, 1985).

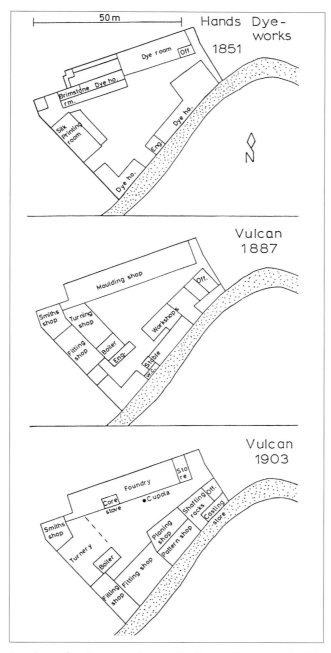

8 Successive plans of a Coventry factory. In the medieval period, this large plot beside the river Sherborne (in the middle of the city) was not built over, probably because it flooded from time to time; it then carried tenters for stretching cloth, and in 1835 was still a garden, with an enormous hot-house. It was then developed as a dye-works by Richard Hands, and in the 1880s became the Vulcan foundry. Redrawn from N. W. Alcock, 'Coventry Streets; West Orchard and the Sherborne', *Trans. Birmingham and Warwickshire Archaeol. Soc.* 91 (1986), 84.

distant communities as shown by migrations and marriages. Typically, the evidence comes from parish registers and wills. However, one particular type of deed, the settlement, is directly concerned with families and their relationships. The marriage settlement was drawn up before (or sometimes shortly after) marriage. It gives the names, occupations and places of residence of husband and wife, generally with details of their parents. Trustees are included, who are either friends or members of the two families involved. The property they hold on behalf of the married couple is, of course, described, and it is not uncommon to find details of the parents' own marriage settlement 20 or 30 years earlier (with their parents' and relatives' names).

Family settlements were usually drawn up once every generation, perhaps when the eldest son came of age.[17] They give details of the family as it existed at that moment, listing the property or money that was earmarked for each child. They also often include information on the preceding settlement. The people involved in big family settlements (Illus. 4) were almost always substantial landowners, gentry at the very least, but marriage settlements are also found for people of very modest status, perhaps owning just a cottage.

POST-MEDIEVAL EVIDENCE

Other deeds contain evidence of family relationships, to an extent that may not always be appreciated. At a rough estimate, from the 18th century onwards, one in every three or four conveyances of property includes some genealogical information (with rather less in leases and mortgages). Such evidence is less frequent in earlier deeds, but it can be even more important because of the lack of other sources; almost invariably deeds will also identify the occupation or social status of the individuals mentioned.[18] Finding the deeds relating to a particular family is often more difficult than finding register entries or wills and, of course, there is no guarantee that the evidence actually exists. Success depends partly on what indexes are available, partly on persistence, and partly on luck—first that the information was recorded in deeds and second that they have survived and can be located; all this is examined in detail in the next chapter. However, the amount of genealogical information in deeds is so great that overall the chances of its discovery are much better than they might seem at first sight.

Family history was included in deeds for very much the same reason as uniform descriptions of the property—so that there could be no doubt of the continuity from one deed to another. Generally, this involved demonstrating that the person or people selling the property were fully entitled to do so. If the owner had bought it himself, no problem arose, but it was not usually considered sufficient just to state that he had been in undisputed possession for many years (in contrast to the present day, when a period of 15 years' ownership is all that has to be proved). Thus one common statement

---

[17] For a full discussion of their interpretation and their significance for English landed estates, see B. English and J. Saville, *Strict Settlement: a Guide for Historians* (University of Hull, 1983).

[18] This was required by the Statute of Additions of 1413, though indications of status remain relatively rare until the 16th century.

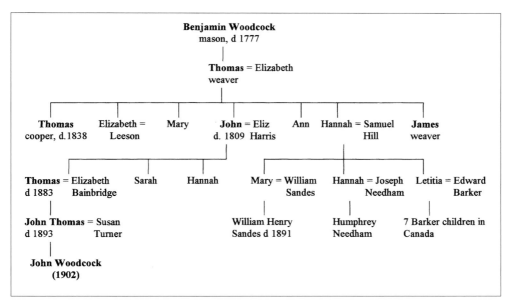

9 Woodcock family tree, 1777–1902. Bold type indicates the direct male descendants of Benjamin Woodcock. [Deed bundle for 49 St John's Street, Coventry; Coventry City Council, Deed Bundle 1229]

in deeds is that the seller's father (or grandfather as the case may be) had held the property. If it had been bequeathed by will so much the better. This gave a particularly strong proof of ownership and was often used as a starting point in establishing title. Another situation in which deeds include particularly good information on family relationships is the inheritance of a property by a number of co-owners. This could arise through someone dying *intestate* (without making a will), leaving only daughters who would by common law inherit equally. Occasionally, property was left by will in equal shares, say to all the testator's grandchildren. In either case one owner could only sell his share, so we find deeds for an 'undivided fifth' of a house. Alternatively, if the property was sold complete, everyone who owned a share had to be a party to the transaction. As an example, deeds for the sale for 49 St John's Street, Coventry in 1902, gives the complete descent to that date of Benjamin Woodcock of Coventry, mason, who died in 1777 (Illus. 9). This is an extreme case (though not unique), because often the practical inconveniences of co-ownership led either to the property being sold fairly soon, or to one owner buying out the shares of the others.

In general, the tracking down and the legal confirmation of heirs must have given lawyers much profit. Complete bundles of title deeds very often contain evidence of their work in the form of baptism, marriage and burial certificates extracted from registers, or sworn statements setting out relationships; actual family trees are quite common, though they usually only cover three or four generations. The earliest pedigree I have ever seen dated from the late 15th century; it was drawn up to explain the descent of a Coventry property from the 1420s through an extremely complicated series of marriages and remarriages. It is now part of a group of family papers, but comparison with the related deeds shows that they originally belonged together. Regrettably the fate of these slips of paper is often to be thrown away as of no value if the deed bundles are broken up and the deeds themselves sold.

It may seem that the use of deeds to establish family relationships is unnecessary, because the parish registers can provide the evidence more easily. Often this may be so, but family historians will know that registers are not without their difficulties, even allowing for the many which have not survived. It only needs a slight problem to break a line—a trifling accident like a man dying intestate away from home, or idleness like that of Edward Agborow, vicar of Stoneleigh, Warwickshire, who from 1679 to his death in 1691 did not touch his registers. Deeds may well provide the means to bridge such gaps. They may also show that people are not always who they seem. In 1719, William Parker (I) of Oxhill, Warwickshire died, leaving his farm in the village to his son William (II). In 1797 William Parker (III) in his turn bequeathed the same property to his son William (IV). Even without any extra evidence, it seems clear that William (III) must either be William (II) himself or his son. Unfortunately, the obvious is not correct. In a deed of 1766, William (II), identified as the son of William (I) and described as of Stratford-upon-Avon, sells his Oxhill inheritance to another William Parker (perhaps a cousin, though this is not stated), and it is this William who died in 1797.[19]

Deeds can also be very helpful in identifying migrants and emigrants, if they owned or inherited property. Sometimes we get unusual detail. A Kenilworth, Warwickshire deed bundle contains a sad letter of 1774 from John Ireland, a soldier serving with the East India Company, explaining that his fellow recruit William Riley, who had inherited a farm in the parish, had died of cholera.[20] The hazards of life overseas, and the difficulties of communication are sometimes explicitly recognised in wills in bequests (not usually of property) to 'my son John who is beyond the seas, if he shall return'. A more typical example of emigrants owning property comes from a fairly recent deed for a house in Kenilworth. It was being sold by the children of the deceased owner, William Skutt of Turua, Auckland, New Zealand, and Henry Skutt of Mint Spring, Virginia, U.S.A. On a local scale, the William Parker (I) mentioned above had bought his Oxhill property in 1690 from Ann Parker, widow and her son Richard Parker, gardener, both of Chelsea; Ann's husband had lived in Oxhill.

Looked at in reverse, finding a deed relating to a particular emigrant may be even more difficult than finding parish register entries, but when found one can be very confident that the right person has been identified. It is relevant to remember that statements in deeds were made with legal care, so that their accuracy could be defended in a law court if necessary; inconsistencies are found in such matters as the spelling of Christian and surnames, but deeds are generally of a better standard than many registers. Children in a family are usually only mentioned if they survive to adulthood, but they are the most important for genealogy, and the entries in a register for those who died young may be a source of confusion rather than clarification.

[19] Shakespeare Birthplace Trust Record Office, ER3/4491-4.
[20] Shakespeare Birthplace Trust Record Office, DR18/10/10/776.

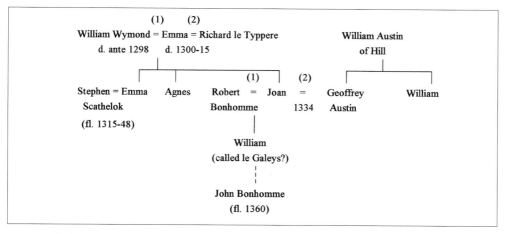

10 Family links between the Wymond and Austin families in early 14th-century Coventry. [From N. W. Alcock, 'The Catesbys in Coventry; a medieval estate and its archives', *Midland History*, XV (1990), 1-36]

MEDIEVAL EVIDENCE

In the medieval period, it is usually fairly easy to establish the pedigree for someone of 'manorial' status, who held at least one manor (preferably directly from the Crown, so that *inquisitions post mortem* abound).[21] Indeed, minor gentry living on their single manor and owning perhaps a farm or two elsewhere, were probably the most stable families in medieval society, sometimes showing little change in their situation for two or three hundred years. Below that social level, migration, changing family names, and the lack of sources make the tracing of family relationships extremely difficult. A long series of manor court rolls undoubtedly gives the best evidence,[22] but these are extremely rare. Title deeds are far more common, though we can be certain that nothing like a complete set ever survives; quite large (sometimes very large) groups do exist for many places, and these provide evidence about a vast number of families. It is necessary to remember that title deeds never existed for some property and some people. In principle, deeds related only to land held by free tenure (of one form or another), rather than villein tenure (whose transfers were recorded in the manor court), owned by free men rather than villeins. This limitation is not as severe as might be supposed, partly because it was not always respected.[23] Furthermore most manors contained some free holdings and some had hardly anything else,[24] while town property, held by *burgage tenure*, could always be transferred by deed.

Two or three individual deeds are all that is needed to reveal a short family tree, but one that can be very complex; indeed, the complexity is often the reason for the information having been recorded. Illustration 10 shows a short medieval family

---

[21] The inquiries made by the Crown to establish the heir of the deceased, and what property he had held; they are in the Public Record Office.

[22] Z. Razi, *Life, Marriage and Death in a Medieval Parish: Economy, Society and Demography in Halesowen, 1270-1400* (Cambridge University Press, 1980).

[23] Discussed in C.N.L. Brooke and M.M. Postan (eds.), *Carte Nativorum*, Northamptonshire Records Society, vol.20 (1960).

[24] Especially woodland manors, where the land was cleared in the post-Conquest period, e.g. Tanworth-in-Arden, Warwickshire; see Baker and Butlin, *op. cit.* in note 2, pp.226-7.

tree from Coventry, which has a particular value for local history in demonstrating that property belonging to William Wymond passed to Robert Bonhomme (in his wife's right), which explains why a lane called Wymond Lane was later known as Bonhomme Lane. The descent to John Bonhomme is not directly mentioned in the deeds, but is deduced because in 1359 he received a rent of six shillings that was formerly paid to William. Such indirect evidence often has to be used for lack of anything better, though its dangers are obvious.

Similar correlations may also help circumvent the worst problems of medieval family history, changing names and migration. For both, it is vital to look not only at the actual owners of property, but at people holding adjoining tenements. An example given later (p.90) shows how a series of fluctuating references identify four names (Robert de London, Robert de Kenilworth, Robert le Keu, and Robert Coki—the cook) as one individual. Similarly, if a property is recorded as belonging to someone from elsewhere, this probably resulted from migration, as people living outside a community hardly ever bought property within it. The exact relationship to a previous resident owner may not be straightforward, but could for example involve inheritance by a sister who had married an outsider.

In working out such problems, the medieval rules of inheritance can sometimes be of help. Although freehold property could be bought and sold, before 1540 land that had been inherited could not be left by will, but descended according to fixed rules. Almost always, inheritance went to the eldest son, though occasionally it followed local custom, either *borough English* (descent to the youngest son), or *gavelkind* (equal division between sons). Daughters were next in line after sons, sharing equally, followed by brothers in order and sisters (divided). If more distant relatives had to be found, the result was often a law suit between people with roughly equal claims. A widow had the right to one third of the property (her 'dower') but for life only, so that if the son sold it with her agreement, she would renounce her right in a *quitclaim* (pp.80, 91). If she herself made a *gift* (p.89), then she had certainly inherited the property herself, rather than holding it as her dower.

PEOPLE IN THE COMMUNITY

Deeds contain most information about the owners of property, but this is not as serious a limitation as might be feared, as many people of humble status owned a little land, such as a cottage and field. By contrast, wealthy yeoman families might rent their farm for generation after generation, perhaps with a series of three-life leases which gave reasonably secure tenure (p.59). Fortunately, leases of this particular type are excellent sources of family information and have a good chance of being preserved among the records of the estate owning the farm. In any case, people with money to invest would often buy land, even if they rented their own farm.

Many people other than the buyer and seller are mentioned in deeds. Some are important—trustees for one or another party, mortgagees, people relinquishing a possible claim. Others slip in almost accidentally—occupiers of houses, owners of adjoining property, witnesses. In the medieval period, witnesses were not random, but were chosen firstly from people of importance in the community, and secondly from near neighbours who could confirm the boundaries and details of the property. The final witness was usually the clerk or scribe who drew up the deed. Thus, almost everybody in the community, down to the occupier of an 18th- or 19th-century slum cottage, was likely to be recorded in deeds on one occasion or another. The limitation of many documentary sources to adult males and widows does not apply strongly to deeds. Wives were often named with their husbands as buyers or sellers, as well as occurring in marriage settlements, while children, young and old, are found in three life leases and in family settlements.

Viewed as sources of information about an individual, deeds contribute many small items, and some larger ones. One of the most significant is the acquisition of property, perhaps enlarging a main farm, buying houses for their rental value or to develop their sites, or perhaps only at second hand, through mortgages. Although a will may list property (though not invariably), deeds are essential to show how an estate was built up, and at what cost, and whether there were disposals as well as acquisitions. Were the purchases within the community, or was he investing elsewhere, either by choice or because nothing was available locally? As the reverse of this, was property in a village or town passing through the hands of people primarily from inside or outside the community?

The network of relationships—family, friendship, business association and profes-sional service—makes up a vital part of the individual character of a village or town, but is the most difficult to identify and describe. It is revealed in the specific links in deeds, buyers with sellers, business men with their partners, mortgagors with mortgagees, trustees with those whose property they hold in trust. These links (supplemented with evidence from other sources) can be drawn out on paper, perhaps with heavier and lighter lines joining the names according to the strength of the connection, to show the community as a working organism (Illus.11). Such diagrams are complicated, but effectively reflect the character of a village or town. In particular, they can reveal any sub-groups it contains, corresponding to political, social, or religious alignments. For individuals, the most important feature of deeds in comparison to other evidence is that they relate to people in the fullness of life, not only at the turning points of birth, marriage, and death. For the family historian, the activities recorded in deeds build up rounded portraits of the names on the family tree, identifying their friends, and even allowing insights into their character and into their approach to life and business. This surely must be the aim of anyone seriously interested in chronicling the history of a family. For the local historian, this same rounding out of individuals who are otherwise just names on a tax list, or passing members of a town's administration, enables him to assess their roles, and

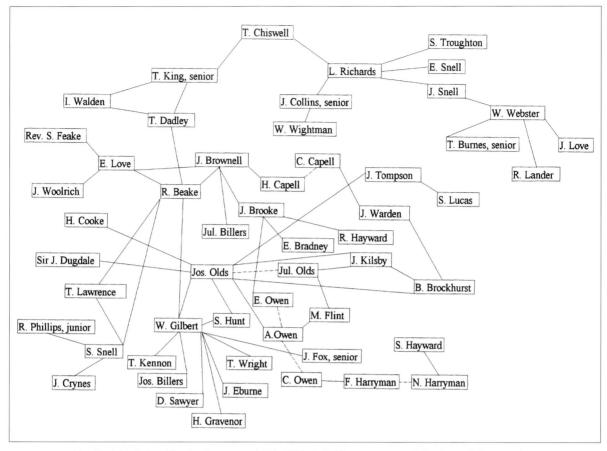

11   Social relationships in Coventry, 1680–1700. Solid lines represent links derived from probate evidence and dashed lines indicate family relationships. [Unpublished work by J. Hunt.]

perhaps to pick out those people in the past who were key figures in the growth of the community, or in its decline. In this way, deeds add a human dimension to the description of places and happenings.

PEOPLE IN COPYHOLD DEEDS AND MANOR COURT ROLLS

If you find that the people you are researching are recorded in a copyhold deed (holding property by copy of court roll (p.94), or that they lived on a manor for which court rolls survive (fortunately true for very many places in England), then you should be able to discover a considerable amount about the family. This is particularly true if they held copyhold property (even if only a cottage), but the standard entries in the rolls will also help to provide a rounded view of their place in village society; they may have transgressed against village orders, overstocking the common lands, or leaving dung heaps in

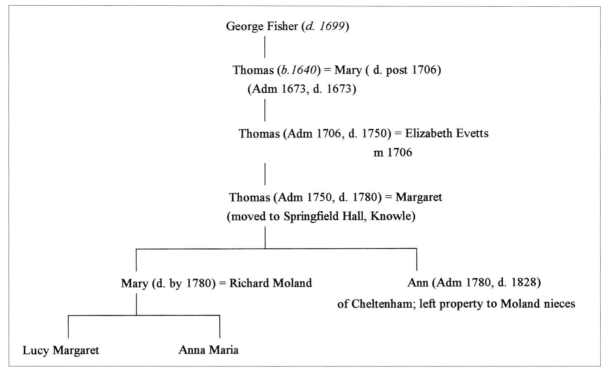

12 Fisher family tree, 1640-1828. [From court rolls for Temple Balsall, Warwickshire (WRO CR112) and parish registers for Barston, Warwickshire] Adm=Admitted to property.

the street, or they may have served as jurors on the court, as constables, ale tasters or other village officials. Property deeds for copyhold land (copies of court roll) are often found in deed bundles, but the original court rolls can be particularly informative if they can be found, as these may well contain additional information. Their value was brought home to me when I was tracing a family called Fisher, living in Barston, Warwickshire. The principal problem was that the parish contained a whole shoal of Fishers. No less than six received allocations in the 1734 enclosure award, and one single court book for 1727-49 has 31 Fisher items, while the parish registers contain innumerable possibly relevant entries. My study started with Ann Fisher, spinster, the owner of a Barston house in 1818, when she was then living in Cheltenham. Following her family back through the court books readily produced the tree in illustration 12, from George Fisher who built the family house and his son Thomas who died well before his father, through to Ann, the last of the line, dying in 1828. Most important, because the court entries could be associated through the property descriptions (and often included the date of the previous entry), I was completely confident that the tree was correct; it was then easy to add some additional information from the parish registers.

DEEDS AND COMPUTERS

With the many hundreds of deeds that may refer to a particular place, or be relevant to a particular investigation, using a computer for their interpretation can be a great help—or it can swallow up time and effort to produce nothing at all. What follows may reduce the risk of the latter (and not just by rejecting the computer). The choice of a computer over manual methods depends partly on personal inclination, and on the weight given to the ability to produce the information stored in different ways, rather than retyping it on each occasion. It also depends on just how many deeds are being studied. A simple medieval deed might include five to fifteen items of information (names, places, dates, etc.). Therefore about 100 deeds (i.e. 1,000 separate data items) might be the break-even point between computers and card-indexes for simple tasks mainly involving indexing. More sophisticated analysis may well be difficult by hand, even with fewer items of information, but it is important to consider whether enough evidence is available to give satisfactory answers to the questions being asked (particularly if statistical methods are involved). If in doubt, a trial run with the computer is probably worthwhile; once the initial problems have been overcome, the benefits of using a computer become more and more apparent as the amount of data increases.

It is easy to enthuse about the benefits of using a computer but three hurdles have to be overcome:
  (i)   choosing appropriate equipment—the *hardware*;
  (ii) finding useful *software*, the computer programs to manipulate the data—and perhaps even writing one's own programs;
  (iii) *capturing* the data, i.e. typing the information into the computer. The labour and difficulty of this stage is often overlooked by the inexperienced, and here, if anywhere, is where a computer study may founder.

For most people, the obvious hardware will be some form of personal computer (an IBM type PC with Windows or an Apple Mac). Any currently available machine (and most that might be bought second-hand) has more than enough power and memory for any task likely to be encountered in an individual deed-based study. A good quality portable computer (laptop) could be particularly useful, because it can easily be taken into the record office; this has been my personal choice for a number of years.

One other aspect of computer hardware must be emphasised. *They can break down!* It is vital that you make regular back-ups of your data from the computer— usually on a floppy disk, but other methods exist. Back-ups don't take very long and the only satisfactory procedure is to do one *at the end of every working session!*

The most tedious part of a computer-based study is the *data capture*. Before starting on this, it is vital to decide just how the data should be organised, to minimise effort, to avoid duplication during input, and to make the result as easy to use as possible. However, the organisation of the data depends mainly on the type of program to be used.

The simplest approach is to type the complete deed text, or an abstract, into a word-processing program. However, this is only likely to be the best solution if you are planning to publish the deeds themselves (or if you can use a sophisticated plain-text system as described below). Although word-processing programs can be used to search for specific items and will produce indexes (by marking each word to be indexed), they are very restricted in what they can achieve in the way of sorting and selecting particular items.

You can also use a word-processing program with the data structured into the form of a table, or with each name 'flagged' with a marker character (e.g. P1 for the first party). A procedure of this type was described in the first edition, but this approach has really been superseded by the availability of good commercial *database* programs for personal computers. Examples are Microsoft Works or Access, or Corel Paradox. I used Paradox in the study of medieval deeds for the village of Wootton Underwood, Buckinghamshire described below. In the database, each deed is representented by a precisely specified set of items of information (date, names of people concerned, witnesses, etc.). After the data has been entered into the database, the information can be sorted, looked at on screen or printed as a whole or in part, to produce indexes. Some simple statistical analysis is usually possible, but to apply sophisticated techniques, it will probably be necessary to use a specialised program.

The first step in using any database program is to design the form of the database. With most programs, it is possible to alter the form of the database entries after you have started entering the data, but this causes problems, especially if you have to go back and re-examine the original documents to add extra information. So, it is best to work out the database structure, test it on a small sample and then keep it fixed. Table 1 shows the items that were included in the main database for the Buckinghamshire study, with an example of the data.

The information recorded for each entry (deed) is identical. Thus, you have to decide, say, that your deeds will have at most eight witness 'fields', and also that each witness name will take no more than 30 characters. Fortunately, the great increase in the size of hard disks on modern personal computers means that the size of each field no longer needs to be kept as small as possible. This study used the personal names in the documents more than the property information, so the latter was incorporated in a 'memo' field, of variable length; the manipulations that can be done with these fields are limited, so they should not be used for the main data. The problem of dealing with a deed with more witnesses than the eight fields was covered by allowing deeds to be continued in a second record (marked by a Y in the CONT field); these continuation records had to be handled specially in some stages of the processing, but this seemed more satisfactory than doubling the number of witness fields.

A number of deed studies have used databases, often as an aid to indexing.[25] A particularly sophisticated application is in the DEEDS project,[26] a large-scale study

[25] See, for example, J. Blair and P. Riden, 'Computer-assisted analysis of medieval deeds', *Archives*, vol.15 (1982), pp.195-208.
[26] J.L. Kordecki, 'Computer techniques and medieval land transfers: the DEEDS project', *J. Society of Archivists*, vol.7 (1984), pp.299-311.

Field Name	Field Type	Sample data	Comments
IDNO	S	177	Number for each deed (*S type = integer*)
GROUP	A2	OR	OR = original deed; some are CP = copy
			(*A2 type = Alphabetic 2 character field*)
CONT	A1		= Y if continued in next record (same IDNO)
BOX	A8	17/5	Archive reference
REIGN	A6	Ed.I	Standard abbreviations used
DATE	A10	1295-2-13	Converted from regnal year and reversed for sorting
P1	A50	Alice la Zuze	
P2	A50	Peter Spileman of	Wife included, to keep husband and wife associated
		Wodehamme + Margery,w.	
PROP	M96	1/2 ac land + head of	Refers to abuttal names as A1, etc. (*M type = memo*
		meadow adjoining. Bought	*field of variable length*)
		& hold in fee of A1. In	
		Yeytfurlong between A2-A3	
A1	A30	Peter Herein of Wotton(was	Abuttals (owners of adjoining property), as
A2	A30	Elye Herni	indicated in the PROP field. '(was' indicates
A3	A30	James de Rupella	'formerly of' named person
A4	A30		
W1	A30	Peter de Rupella	First witness
W2	A30	John his brother	Need to edit to 'John brother of Peter de Rupella'
W3	A30	Richard de Aula	
W4	A30	Richard de Rupella	
W5	A30	William Walerand	
W6	A30	William Frankeleyn	
W7	A30	Roger de Brehull, clerk	Last witness is a clerk, perhaps the scribe
W8	A30		
HOLD_ME	A1	*	* = property to be held of grantee
HOLD_CHIEF	A1		★ = property to be held of chief lord (see p. xx).
			Here held of former owner, A1
NOTES/	M80	Cons.[*Consideration*] 1 mark	Any other information in deed. Standard
COMMENT		R.[*Rent*] 1d to lord of fee	abbreviations are used to save time during input
		at Ann.[*Annunciation*]	

Table 1 Database study of deeds for Wootton Underwood, Buckinghamshire: Fields used and data for a typical entry.

of medieval Essex deeds. It involved the design of its own database, and the production of special programs to process the information. The data files had a very complex structure, but with most of the parts optional, so that the limitations of a rigid structure were avoided. The software used for DEEDS could certainly be applied to other studies, but one would need access to considerable programming expertise as well as a main-frame computer. Among other applications, the information was used for dating deeds, for identifying changing fashions in property transactions, and for correlating references to particular individuals.

The newest developments are in the direction of simplifying the input procedures but making the processing very sophisticated, by the use of 'mark-up' language (usually that known as SGML). This procedure avoids the compromises inevitable with a database program that imposes a rigid structure on documents of variable form. The first step in this sort of application is to type either an abstract of the deed or its complete text. A typical deed abstract would be:

A10640 [*the reference*]; William Oysel of Coventry conveys to William de Erescote and Edith, wife; tenement in Gosseford Street [*in Coventry*] between house of Henry

Carpenter, house of John Pope, from street to land of Henry Pake; Witnesses: Robert the baker, bailiff; Anketin de Colshull; Peter Barun; Henry Pake; 12 June 1307.

Then an automated editing program is used to embed a series of commands into the text, identifying the different sections of the text; Table 2 provides a complete example from a study in progress on medieval deeds for Oxford.[27] In the text file, each item or section of the text is bracketed by a pair of markers, e.g. <*WITNESSES*> and </*WITNESSES*>. These can also include qualifiers, e.g. <*PERSON persid=WBicester*> to identify one of the witnesses by a standard form of their name. The types of markers and their qualifiers were set up at the start of the project to be part of an editing program which inserts many of the mark-up commands semi-automatically into the plain text of the deed. The final deed text with its markers result is very like a 'web page' on the World Wide Web, which uses the similar mark-up language HTML. By using a viewer (similar to Netscape), what is seen on the screen is just the text, but the mark-up commands allow the viewer to highlight sections in different colours and provide information for generating indexes, etc.

APPLICATIONS OF COMPUTER DATA

The simplest use of computer data files, whether they take the form of plain text, database files or SGML marked-up files, is for sorting and indexing. This is one of the most valuable ways in which the computer can help historical research. For example, the production of a personal name index from a database file should be easy to achieve. Sorting and selecting items from the file is also very useful, collecting for example all the references to a specific street or hamlet, or isolating all the deeds produced within a certain date range. However, these indexes may run into snags, particularly because medieval names were often very variable, not only in their spelling but also in the application of completely different names to the same people or the same places. The reverse of this is also very common, the same name applying to different people. For example, in the study of Wootton Underwood deeds, one of the lords of the manor, William de Grenville, had his surname spelt in at least ten ways (Grenevil, Grenevile, Grenevill, Grenevyle, Greneville, Grenvile, Grenvyle, Greynvil, Greynville, Greynvylle), and in addition was given as William Grenevylle and William *le* Grenevile (with further surname variants); William the brother of John de Grenevyle and a William the son of Richard Greynvile were also listed, who might or might not have been the same person. It has been my experience that sorting by *first* rather than *last* name is more useful for identifying individuals, because first names have much more standardised spellings. This also makes it easy to recognise variants like William de Grenville and William le Grenville. Starting from such a listing, a number was added to each distinct name (e.g. 607 for William de Grenville, William Grenevylle, etc.); then, to make the index, all the references to name variants with the same number were collected together. My

[27]   This is being carried out by the Oxford Historical Society, under the direction of Tony Dodd, who has kindly provided information on the project and the example used in the figure. The programs will in the future be made available for other studies.

[Reference information] *<!DOCTYPE OES PUBLIC "-//Oxford Historical Society//DTD OES 0.96//EN"> <OESDOC type=charter st=grant id=396 keyed=ed date=040196 rev=2> <SOURCE level=1 docid=OHS70 textid=4> <SOURCE level=2 arcid=university textid='O.26'> <DATE d=25 m=6 y=1320> <TEXT l=latin>*

[Start of deed] *<BODY>* **Sciant presentes & futuri quod ego**

[Party] *<PARTY role=grantor> <PERSON persid=auto mapid=971>* **Iohannes de Trillawe clericus** *</PERSON> </PARTY>*

[Action] *<ACT ty=grant>* **dedi, concessi & hac presenti carta mea confirmavi** *</ACT>*

[Party] *<PARTY role=grantee> <PERSON persid=auto mapid=550>* **magistro Nicholao de Tyngewyke** *</PERSON> </PARTY>*

[Property] *<D> <TENT ty=messuage id=sw70 par=StEbbe>* **unum mesuagium cum pertinenciis in Oxonia situatum in parochia Sancte Ebbe inter** *<ABUTTAL dir=e> <TENT id=sw103>* **tenementum** *<NONPARTY role=neighbour> <PERSON persid=auto mapid='?'>* **Iohannis de Derham** *</PERSON> </NONPARTY> </TENT>* **ex parte orientali** *</ABUTTAL>* **et** *<ABUTTAL dir=w> <TENT id=sw71>* **tenementum** *<NONPARTY role=neighbour> <PERSON persid=auto mapid='?'>* **Willelmi le Wilde** *</PERSON> </NONPARTY> </TENT>* **ex parte occidentali** *</ABUTTAL>* **et** *<ABUTTAL dir=s>* **extendit se versus austrum usque ad murum ville Oxonie et usque ad** *<TENT id=sw69>* **tenementum quondam** *<NONPARTY role=exneighbour> <PERSON persid=hgamage>* **Henrici de Gamage** *</PERSON> </NONPARTY> </TENT> </ABUTTAL> </D>* **;** *</BODY>*

[Tenure] *<HABENDUM>* **habendum et tenendum totum mesuagium antedictum cum omnibus pertinenciis suis quibuscumque prefato Iohanni de Trillowe, heredibus et assignatis suis libere, quiete, integre, bene et in pace de capitalibus dominis feodi illius per servicia inde debita et de iure consueta imperpetuum pro omni servicio.** *</HABENDUM>*

[No warranty] *<WARRANTY> &warranty; </WARRANTY>*

[Consideration] *<CONSID sum=unknown>* **Pro hac autem donacione dedit michi predictus magister Nicholaus quandam summam pecunie pre manibus.** *</CONSID>*

[No sealing information] *<SEALING> &sealing1; </SEALING>*

[Witnesses] *<WITNESSES>* **hiis testibus,** *<NONPARTY role=witness> <PERSON persid=IHampton off=mayor>* **Iohanne de Hamptone tunc maiore Oxonie,** *</PERSON> </NONPARTY>* , *<NONPARTY role=witness> <PERSON persid=Mimecan off=bailiff>* **Rogero Mimecan** *</PERSON> </NONPARTY>* **et** *<NONPARTY role=witness> <PERSON persid=HEdrop off=bailiff>* **Henrico de Edrope** *</PERSON> </NONPARTY>* **tunc ballivis eiusdem ville,** *<NONPARTY role=witness> <PERSON persid=IDuck>* **Iohanne de Dokelintone** *</PERSON> </NONPARTY>* , *<NONPARTY role=witness> <PERSON persid=WBicester>* **Willelmo de Burcestre** *</PERSON> </NONPARTY>* , *<NONPARTY role=witness> <PERSON persid=IColeshull>* **Iohanne de Coleshulle** *</PERSON> </NONPARTY>* , *<NONPARTY role=witness> <PERSON persid=IAurifaber2>* **Iohanne le Orfeuere** *</PERSON> </NONPARTY>* , *<NONPARTY role=witness> <PERSON persid=auto mapid=78>* **Thoma de Alstone** *</PERSON> </NONPARTY>* , *<NONPARTY role=witness> <PERSON persid=auto mapid=93>* **Roberto de Westone** *</PERSON> </NONPARTY>* **et aliis.** *</WITNESSES>*

[Date] *<DATUM locus=ox parsed=yes>* **Dat' apud Oxoniam die Mercurii proxima post festum Nativitatis sancti Iohannis Baptiste anno regni regis Edwardi filii regis Edwardi terciodecimo.** *</DATUM> </TEXT> </OESDOC>*

Table 2 Fourteenth-century Oxford deed with SGML mark-up (text kindly provided by Tony Dodd). The text of the deed itself is in bold type, the mark-up commands in italics between < >, and comments are in brackets[ ]. For the general structure of such medieval deeds, see p.86.

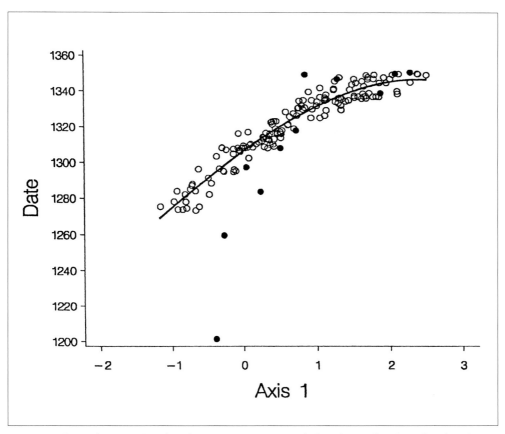

13 Correlation between 'similarity' (score on Axis 1) and date for medieval Buckinghamshire deeds. Solid dots identify 'outliers', which are known to be weakly related to the bulk of the deeds. [F.D. Neiman and N.W. Alcock, 'Archaeological Seriation by Correspondence Analysis: An Application to Historical Documents', *History and Computing*, 7 (1995), 1-21.]

policy for dealing with possible duplicate names has been to assume initially that all occurrences of the same name refer to one person, and only split them at a later stage when all the information about their date, etc. is available. However, names with distinguishing features are treated as different, e.g. separating William de Grenville and William the son of Richard Greynville (on the grounds that the latter name was used for a particular reason). Again, when more knowledge of the family has been obtained, it will be possible to decide if these two are actually the same.

Among more complicated procedures is statistical analysis—counting numbers of deeds of particular types or relating to particular places, or discovering whether two items (two people, say) tend to occur together (correlation analysis). Linked items can also be extracted and displayed, for example identifying all the references to a particular person, together with the place where he lived and the date of the item.[28] This can

---

[28] Examples of all these applications are given in Kordecki, *op.cit.* in note 26.

also help to distinguish different people of the same name and suggest the date of an undated medieval deed, by finding the occurrences of the people it names.

Detailed statistical analysis was applied in the Wootton Underwood study.[29] This used a large group of deeds in the Henry E. Huntington Library, San Marino, California, and the principal objective was to try to assign dates to the 148 undated deeds, by comparison to the 171 deeds with pre-1350 dates (319 deeds in all). The statistical procedure known as 'correspondence analysis' was applied, using as data a large matrix (319 rows x 691 columns), where the presence or absence in one particular deed of each of the 691 distinct names was indicated by 1 or 0. Values for the 'similarity' between any two deeds were derived from this matrix and these values were then used to position the deeds on a set of three axes. For the *dated* deeds, the position along the first of these axes shows a very close correlation with the date (Illus.13). The corresponding position of each *undated* deed then gives a good indication of its date, with an estimated error of no more than five years. Variation along the other axes was much smaller, but one group of deeds showed up as a distinct cluster at the end of Axis 3. These were found to involve people from the adjoining parish of Westcote who owned land in Wootton and tended to witness the same deeds. Thus, this statistical technique is capable of re-creating historical neighbourhood groups from the apparently unpromising deed witness lists.

An extension of this analysis would be to extract sections of the matrix for, say, successive time periods of 30 years (to allow for people coming into prominence and then retiring or dying). From these blocks, groups of associated individuals could be identified. This would generate a picture of community links and relationships similar to that shown in illustration 10. Clearly, the technique will be most effective with the greatest amount of data, and so information from wills etc. should also be included; such names can be entered into the database in just the same way as deed names.

---

[29] F.D. Neiman and N.W. Alcock, 'Archaeological Seriation by Correspondence Analysis: An Application to Historical Documents', *History and Computing*, 7 (1995), 1-21. See also 'Archaeology' in *Encyclopaedia of Statistical Sciences* (Wiley, 1982), vol.I (and the references given there), and C. Orton, *Mathematics in Archaeology* (Collins, 1980), pp.47, 81. Seriation techniques have been used in archaeology, but to my knowledge this is the first application to historical studies.

3

WHERE?

Before deeds can be used as historical evidence, they have to be located. This chapter considers what to look for, and where to look. Sometimes the deeds are easy to find, collected in the most obvious local record office, but they can be scattered—in other record offices, in national collections, in private hands, or even in American, Australian, or Canadian libraries. Some of the collections are partly or completely indexed, but these indexes themselves may not be easily accessible. It is important to be as thorough as possible, because the odd stray deed in an American library might be the vital link in locating a medieval street, or connecting two parts of a family tree. Unfortunately, checking all possible locations is hardly practical even for the most dedicated researcher. We can only hope that better indexes will become available in the future, perhaps through the energies of the growing army of family historians.

For the historian using deeds, three types of index are valuable. The first two are straightforward and are provided in most record offices. Place indexes list the deeds by the places to which they relate, preferably with their dates. Person indexes list those named in the deeds (though they rarely include minor people like former owners or witnesses). If these indexes are to be of any help in recognising individuals, they need also to include the place where the person lived and the date of the reference. The third index is again a place index but for individuals, e.g. to Thomas Brown of Stretton-under-Fosse. Unfortunately, this information tends either not to be indexed at all, or to be combined with a standard place index; this confuses topographical studies by diluting the specific references with more general ones. When such an index does exist independently, it is particularly useful, both to local historians for showing the wider connections of the community, and to family historians for building up a picture of the society into which their family fits. Of these indexes, most record offices manage the first fairly well, sometimes blended with the third, but good personal indexes are much rarer. We should compliment the few record offices that provide excellent indexes (such as the Shakespeare Birthplace Trust Record Office, Stratford-on-Avon), and hope that our research frequently takes us to them.

WHAT TO LOOK FOR

THE LOCAL HISTORIAN
Obviously the local historian will look for deeds relating to the parish or town with which he is concerned. It is important not to be too precise in setting the limits. A

simple precaution is to check for hamlets and subsidiary settlements, which are not always cross-referenced under the parish name; this is particularly relevant for medieval deeds. It can also be useful to range further afield, though the practicality of this strategy varies with the amount of material to be covered, and with its difficulty of access. Farms in one parish not uncommonly lap over into another (and the small component sometimes escapes the indexer's attention), while individuals can have very scattered property holdings. Following up the latter line of enquiry is perhaps more important for the family historian.

When scanning lists of places, it is wise to collect even peripheral references, to avoid the need to repeat the search. Similarly, if a bundle of deeds has been located in some out-of-the-way library or solicitor's office, it is worthwhile to record it in as much detail as possible, even if it does not fit in immediately with the project under way. At a later stage you may well find such items assuming new significance.

THE FAMILY HISTORIAN'S OBJECTIVES

Virtually all deed collections are indexed principally by place, and personal indexes often fail to distinguish individuals of the same name. Thus the family historian has a more difficult task than the local historian in finding his evidence. Unless the family name is extremely rare, a simple search by name will find a lot of irrelevant facts, while probably missing vital ones. The first step has to be to place the family in its village or town, from parish registers, wills, census records, etc. Deeds can then fill in the family links, its prosperity and property ownership, its social background, and relationships with neighbours.

The family historian therefore has almost the same requirement as the local historian, to find deeds relating to a particular place, though the information he wants from them is rather different. He may be able to concentrate on a specific period, though this may change with new information. It is important not to restrict the study, say, to deeds in which a member of the family is purchaser or seller, as important evidence may come from the names of tenants or owners of adjoining properties.

WHERE TO LOOK

LOCAL COLLECTIONS

The obvious places to start the search for title deeds are in the appropriate county record offices. Frequently, these are not the only substantial collections of local records in the county. For example, in Nottinghamshire the University of Nottingham has major collections while the Shakespeare Birthplace Trust Record Office, Stratford-upon-Avon, complements the Warwickshire County Record Office; and the area of the West Midlands is also served by Coventry City Record Office and Birmingham Reference Library. The latter deserves special mention. It has been collecting records since 1866, though almost all its holdings were destroyed in 1879 (and lists of what was lost then make tantalising reading). Since then, however, it has acquired immense numbers of deeds and other records, not merely for Birmingham itself but for the three adjoining counties and many more scattered places.[1]

As a general principle, all the local record offices should be checked for parishes in a particular county, as there is rarely much logic to where collections have arrived—nor are duplicate card indexes as common as they might be. Record offices are listed in two publications. The Royal Commission on Historical Manuscripts produces *Record Repositories in Great Britain* (H.M.S.O., 11th edition, 1999). *British Archives* by Janet Foster and Julia Sheppard (Macmillan, 1995; 1,109 entries) includes some semi-private and specialist collections, and also several locations whose holdings are recorded as 'none'. It covers a number of places with local records and deeds which are omitted from *Record Repositories*. Both these are effectively superseded by a full listing of record repositories on the ARCHON web site (http://www.hmc.gov.uk/archon/archon.htm). This includes addresses, phone numbers and links to the organisation's own web site (if any); it includes a number of overseas libraries that hold British archives.

OUT-COUNTY RECORDS

It is very rare for record offices not to provide some deeds for any parish in their area, but equally rare for them to have all those that survive. The next sections consider other places that may supplement local collections. All too often, even if the deeds exist, finding them is a matter of luck because of a lack of proper aids. All record offices include what is known as 'out-county' material. Sometimes this has arrived by chance, with no real local connection, but more often it relates to isolated property owned by someone whose main interests are in another locality. Occasionally, such collections have been divided between different record offices when major sections relate to widely separated areas; an example is the archives of the Dukes of Bedford, split between the Bedfordshire and the Devon Record Offices. More often such collections have been kept as a unit.

Record offices tend to neglect out-county material in favour of more local documents—natural but regrettable as one area's undervalued out-county document can be of vital interest in another. Their place indexes can be expected to include out-county documents and normally these are organised by county, so that the related documents and places can be easily located. A few, shamefully, have only a single sequence of places in- and out-county, making the location of, say, Warwickshire material almost impossible. No doubt they have a significant proportion of mis-identifications as well (always a hazard with unfamiliar material). The archivists must surely realise how unsatisfactory this arrangement is, but have perhaps not considered the very modest effort needed to reorganise the index—merely to run through it and refile the out-county cards under their own counties. It is also worth

---

[1] Readers should be warned that several thousand of their deeds are not covered in their main chronological and place index, and the only way of access to them is to scan the two enormous accession registers which give a scanty list of places. Happily, recataloguing of the earlier accessions is now under way, though it will take a considerable time before this is complete.

suggesting at this point how desirable it is for books covering material from many scattered places (e.g. calendars of national records) to provide a place index broken down by county; a researcher with regional or local interests would then need only to consult one section with a glance at the 'unidentified' list as well. This was the practice in the Index Library volumes of wills proved in the Prerogative Court of Canterbury, but regrettably is very rare in other published lists.

Finding out-county material is not easy, unless a major landowner can be identified and the location of the family archives discovered. Very few record offices take the obvious step of passing on information about all their out-county holdings. The only systematic method is the laborious one of either writing to or visiting all the record offices in the country, and then perhaps repeating the process a few years later in relation to some other place. This is rather impractical, and not well received by county archivists who dislike being bombarded with apparently random requests. It is often useful to visit adjoining counties, which are the most likely to hold relevant documents, and it is of course worthwhile enquiring of record offices believed to contain specific estate collections with local connections. If the archives of an estate that is of interest cannot be located, the National Register of Archives, London may provide the answer. They hold some 30,000 reports describing individual collections, mainly prepared by record offices. The list of their reports can be searched on-line, by family name or title, and by name for businesses and organisations, but to see the reports themselves you have to visit the NRA or the record office holding the collection.

The solution to the problem of locating out-county documents would be a union index covering everything relating to a particular county not in the county record office or other specified record offices. Regrettably, no such index exists. The National Register of Archives would be the obvious organisation to undertake this, though at present they have no real place index.

NATIONAL COLLECTIONS

Two places in London (the Public Record Office and the British Library) and one in Wales (the National Library of Wales, Aberystwyth) have collections of deeds on a national scale, and may well hold deeds related to any given place in England or Wales. The Bodleian Library, Oxford, and the Cambridge University Library have superb holdings of manuscripts, but include substantial, rather than enormous, numbers of deeds. These relate principally, though not exclusively, to the Midlands and East Anglia respectively. Both libraries have indexes of places but not people. The Bodleian Library's holdings are calendared in W.H. Turner and H.O. Coxe, *Calendar of Charters and Rolls preserved in the Bodleian Library* (Oxford, 1878), continued on microfiche in Bodleian Library, *Calendars of charters and rolls in the manuscript collections of the Bodleian Library* (Chadwyck-Healey, 1992); unfortunately very few libraries hold copies of either of these calendars. Because the National Library of Wales was founded many years before any of the Welsh county record offices, its manuscript holdings include much material, estate archives, solicitors deposits, parish records, etc. that might elsewhere be in county offices. It has a place index. The library is clearly an essential place to look for deeds relating to anywhere in Wales. It also has some English material, mainly derived from Welsh landowners with property in England. Cardiff Central Library also collected material for the whole of Wales, and its archive holdings are now in Glamorgan County Record Office.[2]

The Manuscript Division of the British Library has a large holding of deeds, many of them medieval; they are arranged in various series—Harleian Charters, Additional Charters etc. depending on when and how they were acquired—but these series are of no significance for the type of deed. They are indexed in an enormous series of index volumes which include both people and places in a single sequence. This index is based on the printed accession lists, and is therefore far from comprehensive. However, the library also has calendars (brief descriptions) of most of its deeds; separate and more comprehensive place and personal indexes to these are to be found in the Reading Room. None of the indexes cover recent accessions (which include some deed collections), but a consolidated computerised index is now available.

The Public Record Office holds deeds in overwhelming numbers and frankly overwhelming confusion in more than sixty different classes. Optimists should be warned that there is nothing approaching a single index, whether of people or of places, and many classes are still entirely unindexed; a major advance is that their computer catalogue covers the personal and place names in the lists that already exist. Some of the indexes exist only in single copies in the P.R.O. search rooms, where they can be located from the card indexes arranged by class; others are in the IND series, and have to be called up like other documents. Some indexes have been published in the List and Index Society volumes (copies in most university libraries and some record offices). Because it often does not take long to abstract a deed, it is useful to know that if one is working with deed classes in which every deed has to be requested separately, the normal limit of three documents at one time can be by-passed by writing to the P.R.O. in advance with a list of the deeds one wishes to see.

Table 3 gives a list of the P.R.O. classes that contain deeds, based on the published Guide to the Public Record Office (H.M.S.O., 1963). It also shows the number of items, their date range, and the availability of lists or indexes.

The most important P.R.O. deed groups need further comment. The majority of the medieval deeds were collected at the end of the last century into a series of artificial classes known as Ancient Deeds (containing about 60,000 deeds in all). Evidence of their original source or arrangement has been lost in the process, except for the division into four major groups, though the provenance of some deeds is clear from internal evidence. The largest group consists of Ancient Deeds series B and D (which belong together). They derive from the archives of the dissolved monasteries

---

[2] Using these national collections is not as easy as visiting a county record office (though the National Library of Wales is least difficult). Reader's tickets are required for them all, and may need to be obtained in advance, so it is wise to write before making a visit; the Bodleian Library and Cambridge University Library make charges for tickets. It is almost impossible to identify the precise references to the documents of interest without visiting the collections, though for the Public Record Office, the volumes published by the List and Index Society may help as may their on-line catalogue. Unfortunately, the Bodleian Library (especially) and the Public Record Office take a long time to produce documents, so a preliminary visit mainly to obtain references may be worthwhile; it is also possible to order documents in advance by letter or telephone.

Ancient Deeds (to 1603)

Each group is identified by letter as well as a class number and each is divided into a main series together with large deeds (AA, etc.), and deeds with fine seals (AS, etc.). One series of non-property deeds has been omitted from this table (E213 (RS), E404, and E481-516). All the main groups (A-E) are completely listed and most of the deeds are included in the *Descriptive Catalogue of Ancient Deeds* H.M.S.O., 6 vols., 1890-1915. These contain indexes to places and principal people (of varying quality). See also List and Index Society, vols. 95, 101, 113, 124, 137, 151-2, 158, 200. Some items are being added to these classes from newly sorted material, so it is worth checking the original lists at the PRO or the computerised catalogue.

Class Number	Number of Deeds	Comments
E40(A)	15910	A-series: Treasury of Receipt
E41(AA)	533	
E42(AS)	545	
E43(WS)	615	Mainly receipts and warrants but includes a few deeds
E101		Bundles 640-660 contain some stray deeds probably from the A-series
E326(B)	12656	B-series: Court of Augmentations (property of dissolved monasteries);
E327(BX)	783	BX deeds were published in Thomas Madox *Formulare Anglicanum*,
E328(BB)	433	1702; E315, vols.29-54 comprise the Cartae Miscellaneae, deeds
E329(BS)	483	bound into volumes (unpublished list);
E315/29-54	6756	
C146(C)	11087	C-series: Chancery
C147(CC)	373	
C148(CS)	171	
E210(D)	11325	D-series: Queen's Remembrancer (similar to B)
E211(DD)	698	
E212(DS)	139	
LR14(E)	1668	E-series: Land Revenue (Crown estates)
LR15(E)	200	
WALE29(F)	516	F-series: Wales and Chester
WALE30(FF)	92	
DURH21(G)	9 boxes	G-series: Durham; no list
PL29(H)	63	H-series: Palatinate of Lancaster
DL25(L)	3651	L-series: Duchy of Lancaster
DL26(LL)	106	
DL27(LS)	331	
DL36	236	Bound, as *Cartae Miscellaneae*
E354(P)	50	P-series: Pipe office (mostly originals of enrolled deeds); P but not PP
E355(PP)	300	listed

Modern Deeds (1603 on)

E44(A)	536	
E330(B)	66	
C149(G)	65 boxes unlisted	
E214(D)	1668	
LR16(E)	14 boxes unlisted	
WALE31(F)	8 boxes	Partly transferred to National Library of Wales

[continues opposite]

Table 3　Deed Classes in the Public Record Office.

Court Exhibits

Several series exist, and most contain a great variety of material as well as deeds. They are generally very incompletely listed.

Class Number	Date Range	Comments
WARD2	12th century to Charles I	4698 documents, list in Deputy Keeper, 6th Report of people and places (ref. numbers superseded; also supplemented by partial additional lists). Some of the Ancient Deeds (above) also seem to emanate from the Court of Wards
E140	post-medieval	Queen's Remembrancer exhibits; 1462 items; 246 bundles
E219	post-medieval	Similar to last, but being added to; currently 720 bundles and single items
C171	14th-19th centuries	Six Clerks series; 54 bundles, listed by case, with a few places named
C103-C114	mostly post-medieval	Chancery Masters' Exhibits. List and Index Society vols. 13-14 gives a complete list by law suit, with a summary place and date list for some classes; fuller lists are in preparation
C115	12th-19th centuries	Duchess of Norfolk's Deeds. About 9,000 deeds, partly listed (IND 23396)
C150	medieval	11 deeds and cartulary of Abbey of St Peter, Gloucester, formerly in C115
J90	16th-19th centuries	Supreme Court Exhibits; 1893 bundles (List and Index Society, vol. 197)
PL12	1795-1860	Palatinate of Lancaster; 17 bundles
[WALE27]		[1 bundle, transferred to National Library of Wales]

[continues on p.38]

Table 3 Deed Classes in the Public Record Office.

and chantries, and it is usually possible to recognise the particular sources. The D-series especially seems to comprise fairly large numbers of deeds from a limited number of archives. For Warwickshire, for example, they relate mainly to the property of Stoneleigh Abbey, Arbury and Monks Kirby Priories, and the chantries at Aston, Birmingham and Erdington. One other large series also has a monastic source. This is the Cartae Miscellaneae, consisting of deeds without their seals, bound into volumes.

Series C is from Chancery, and its deeds presumably relate to lawsuits, though this is not easy to prove; fewer deeds seem to relate to each individual place or estate than in the other series. Some of the A-series deeds derive from confiscated estates, and form very large groups indeed. A particularly notable example is the archive of Robert Catesby, relating to estates in Northamptonshire and Warwickshire, forfeited after the Gunpowder Plot. This has never been precisely enumerated, but appears to represent more than ten per cent of the A-series deeds (1,500+ deeds). Another substantial group relates to Cornish property of the Reskymer family though the reason for these deeds being in Crown hands is unclear.

It is important to realise that the Ancient Deeds are by no means a random collection, and that most derive from fewer individual sources than might be supposed. Thus, the presence or absence of a particular place from the collection has very little to do with its importance in the medieval period. With luck, the Ancient Deeds include a mass of information for a given place, but equally they can be totally unhelpful.

Other Series

Class Number	Date Range	Comments
ADM75	13th century–1931	236 bundles. Greenwich Hospital property. Mainly Kent, and Northern England, including former estates of Earl of Derwentwater (forfeited 1715)
C45	1691–1816	1 bundle; no list, origin unknown
C47	Medieval	Chancery Miscellanea; Bundle 9 (63 items) includes deed transcripts; List and Index Society, vol.7
[COAL1	1548–1850	33 deeds for coal mines; now in Derbyshire and Staffordshire record offices]
CRES38	13th century–1964	Relate to Crown lands; 2,460 deeds, listed
DL14	Henry VIII–Geo III	112 bundles, Duchy of Lancaster, draft leases
DL15	Ed VI–1875	110 bundles, Duchy of Lancaster, counterpart leases
DL47	1572–1715	6 bundles, Savoy, counterpart leases
E116	1578–1715	110 deeds, Chatham, Kent, relating to fortifications
E299	1525–1546	Augmentation Office, counterpart leases
E303	1330–1552	Conventual Leases; 29 portfolios; also in E118 (1 bundle)
E304	Commonwealth	Conveyances of Crown lands
E305	c.1536–53	Deeds for purchase and exchange of Crown lands
E307	Commonwealth	Conveyances of fee-farm rents
E311-2	Hen. VIII–James I	Counterparts of leases, etc.; 58 boxes
F15	1781–1894	10 deeds, Forest of Dean
FEC1	1552–1744	58 bundles. Estates forfeited in 1715. See Records of the Forfeited Estates Commission, H.M.S.0., 1968
IR10	1513–1816	68 deeds; listed
LRR05	16th-century–1917	68 bundles. Mainly deeds required by statute to be deposited; listed
MAF6	1720–1863	47 deeds, Manor of Paglesham, Essex
MAF9	1841–1925	369 boxes. Deeds of enfranchisement of copyhold land; see also MAF20
MT21	1639–1939	468 files, Ramsgate Harbour
SC3	18th-19th centuries	Rolls Estate; (Chancery Lane, London) 147 files
SC4	Charles II, 1720	Crown Grants; 8 deeds
T64	1668–1803	Includes a few deeds for Crown lands
TS21	16th-19th centuries	1370 documents, not all deeds; listed
WORK24	1614–1929	8 boxes
WORK7	1700–1915	Board (then Ministry) of Works; 84 boxes
WORK8	1710–1904	82 boxes

Table 3 Deed Classes in the Public Record Office (continued).

Modern Deeds classes corresponding to the Ancient Deeds were also set up, but they are very much smaller, a few thousand documents in all; they are very incompletely indexed. The sorting of 'Exchequer Miscellanea B', which is at present in progress, is adding some items to both the Ancient and Modern series.

The second important source for deeds (especially post-medieval ones) is the Exhibits, documents produced as evidence in lawsuits but never returned. These contain an immense variety of fascinating material, frequently including deeds. Several series of exhibits survive, relating to the various courts. The largest group is the Chancery Masters' Exhibits, from the Court of Chancery. For the most part, they are still in bundles by lawsuit, grouped according to the relevant 'Six Clerks' office (the subdivisions of the Court of Chancery). Thus, if a particular case is known to be of interest, it is well worth checking for an exhibit. Locating relevant material directly is more difficult: for only a minority of the groups do the lists include even a summary of the places concerned. One exhibit has been given a specific class number (C 115), The Duchess of Norfolk Deeds. These are a remarkable collection that reached the Chancery in the early 19th century, and include the muniments of Llanthony Priory with many early deeds relating to the Welsh borders.

Most of the other P.R.O. deed classes are more closely defined, relating to a specific place or estate. Some form interesting groups, such as the Greenwich Hospital deeds, and the Crown Estate documents, both of which go back to the medieval period.

As well as original deeds, the P.R.O. holds many *enrolled* deeds, i.e. deeds copied onto the rolls of one or other of the royal courts (see next section and Table 4), and also the records of the fictitious lawsuits used for property transfers, Recoveries and Fines, which are described later (p.73).

ENROLLED AND REGISTERED DEEDS

Many copies of deeds were recorded when the deeds were originally written, either to validate them (see p.79) or to give the owners greater security against the original being lost. Such copies do not approach a complete record, but they should not be neglected. Only very recently has compulsory registration at the English Land Registry been required (gradually extended since the beginning of the century), but this only takes effect when property is transferred, so even the Registry does not have complete information on land ownership. This is in contrast to Scotland (see p.2), or the United States where title deeds have been recorded comprehensively in local court-houses from the 17th century onwards.

DEED REGISTRIES

In England, local deed registries were started in the early 18th century in Yorkshire (1704-36) and Middlesex (1708), and also in Ireland in 1708, but attempts to extend their activity to the rest of the country were defeated. For these areas, the registers provide comprehensive sources covering more than two million deeds in each county; all the registers are now in the appropriate record office. Registration was not compulsory, but the advantages of having deeds registered soon became so obvious that few if any eligible deeds were omitted; however, leases for less than 21 years and deeds for copyhold property could not be enrolled. At each registry, when a deed had been signed and sealed, the details were recorded by the registrar in a 'Memorial', and the original deed was endorsed with a note of the date and time it was registered. The registers are not a complete substitute for the originals because the memorials usually only include abstracts: dates, parties, witnesses, and property descriptions, omitting the consideration and any conditions or covenants; from the later 19th century on, they include copies of any plans in the original deeds.[3]

---

[3] For an excellent description, see F. Sheppard and V. Belcher, 'The Deeds Registries of Yorkshire and Middlesex', *J. Soc. Archivists*, vol. 6 (1979-81), pp. 274-86. Registries also exist for the Isle of Man and Jersey and (as already noted) in Scotland, where the land law is very different from England. Surprisingly, the earliest English registry to be established (in 1663) is that covering a 75,000 acre tract in the Fens, which was granted to the Adventurers as recompense for providing the funds for drainage (registers in the Cambridgeshire Record Office). See also Peter Roebuck, 'The Irish Registry of Deeds: a comparative study', *Irish Historical Studies*, 18 (1972), 61-73; the Irish memorials are considerably more detailed than in England, including much more of the information in the deed beyond that noted above.

The indexes to the memorials vary in quality. All the registries have indexes to grantors (usually arranged annually by initial letter but not sorted into precise alphabetical order), but only E and W Yorkshire have indexes to grantees (from 1828 and 1763 respectively). The Middlesex registry has no place index at all, and that for West Yorkshire covers only 1704 to 1786 and 1885 to 1923. It would be an exceptionally valuable aid to local and family historians if these indexes could be made more comprehensive − a very worthwhile task for volunteer work. Despite these qualifications, this mass of material provides a historical source for people and places that should be the envy of anyone concerned with other counties. The registers also provide complete blocks of deeds without any problems of survival that can be used for wide-ranging surveys, for example of variations in the land market.

LOCAL ENROLMENTS

One of the reasons for the failure of attempts in the 18th century to create more deed registries was opposition from various boroughs which claimed already to hold 'Courts of Record' in whose rolls deeds were registered. Although they were successful, these objections were specious as by the 18th century this registration was virtually extinct. In the medieval period, enrolling of deeds was carried out energetically in many boroughs, and several important series survive. G.H. Martin has discussed these enrolments,[4] but no list has been made of those that survive, let alone the boroughs which made them but whose records are lost; the making of enrolled copies can be established from the endorsements applied to the deeds on enrolment. However, for anyone studying either the people or the topography of a borough which has surviving rolls, they provide a major source of evidence. The most important series is that for London, enrolled in the Court of Hustings and starting in 1252. It has some 3,000 entries before the end of the 13th century, and 30,000 for the whole medieval period. Wallingford has the earliest roll (1231-2) which is particularly interesting, as it seems to record oral rather than written transactions; the next roll (1252-3) recites written charters, but no later rolls survive. Another major series comes from Norwich, starting in 1285. A recent study has examined the process of enrolment there.[5] It also applies their evidence to the topographical reconstruction of part of the city, and to the analysis of its trades and economic structure.

The other sets of locally-enrolled deeds are those created following the Statute of Enrolments in 1535. This allowed feoffments to be valid without seizin (p.79) if they were enrolled either in the national courts or before the Clerks of the Peace in each county.[6] Locally, the 'Enrolled Deeds of Bargain and Sale' are included amongst Quarter Sessions records. Their popularity and survival is extremely variable. Thus, for Devon a good series starts in 1536 and includes some 1,300 deeds in the

---

[4] G. H. Martin, 'The Registration of Deeds of Title in the Medieval Borough', in D. A. Bullough and R. L. Storey (eds.), *The Study of Medieval Records* (Oxford, 1971), pp. 151-173.

[5] S. Kelly, E. Rutledge, M. Tillyard, *Men of Property, an Analysis of the Norwich Enrolled Deeds, 1285-1311* (Centre of East Anglian Studies, University of East Anglia, 1983).

[6] The East Riding Deed Registry (but not apparently the other Yorkshire registries) also enrolled deeds as well as registering memorials; these enrolments include more than 170 enclosure awards dating between 1735 and 1847, which would elsewhere have been in Quarter Sessions records.

16th century, while the earliest roll for Essex has only 100 deeds in the date range 1536 to 1624. Again, the rolls for Warwickshire do not survive before 1612, and thereafter are very sparse; curiously, the latest ones consist almost entirely of the sales of former toll houses by disbanded turnpike trusts.

NATIONAL ENROLMENTS

Deeds had been copied onto the rolls of the royal courts at Westminster from the 13th century onwards, [7] and the increasing popularity of this form of record probably provided one stimulus for the Statute of Enrolments. Several series of enrolments are found, within the four 'Courts of Record', and these are listed in Table 4.

Of these series, the most important are the vast numbers of enrolments in the Court of Chancery (Close Rolls), and to a lesser extent those in Common Pleas (Plea Rolls). The latter have lists or indexes of places for the post-medieval period which are relatively easy to search, but the rolls themselves are extremely daunting, piles of parchment sheets bound together at one end, anything up to a foot thick and three feet long. Some of the indexes (but not all) give the membrane number; on all the rolls, the deeds are in a separate section at the end. Feet of Fines (described on p.75) are also records of the Court of Common Pleas, though they are not strictly enrolments of originals. The Plea Rolls and the Recovery Rolls also contain the original enrolled court judgements, whose copies are the Exemplifications of Recoveries (see p.76).

The Close Rolls initially provided a record of letters sent by the King, but this use rapidly declined from the 15th century. The texts of deeds began to be copied onto the backs of the rolls (the dorses) in the 14th century, and this eventually overwhelmed the original purpose, so that only the dorses were written. Enormous numbers of deeds were recorded in the later 16th and 17th centuries, with for example 1,195 rolls (perhaps 75,000 deeds) for the reign of Elizabeth, compared with 206 rolls for the reigns of all the earlier Tudors.[8] The great majority of the enrolments are of deeds, though they include financial arrangements and other matters. By the 18th century, enrolments were declining, until in the 19th century the rolls were used mainly for a few types of deeds, in particular the grants of property to the trustees of charities; these trust deeds have a special index.[8a]

The medieval Close Rolls have been published up to the end of the reign of Henry VII, including the enrolled deeds. After this, unfortunately, the finding aids become very unsatisfactory, just as the number of deeds increases. The only indices are two sets of contemporary year-by-year lists of the grantors and grantees (sellers and purchasers) in the deeds, arranged alphabetically by initial letter, but not sorted for each initial; the indexes give the surnames of both parties, and from 1671 onwards the county is included. The provision of a full index of parties and places for this immense mass of material would be an outstanding aid to historians of all kinds, but seems unlikely to be

---

[7] See S. J. Bailey, 'Thirteenth Century Conveyancing from the Charter Rolls', *Cambridge Law Review*, 1961, 200.

[8] A study of the evidence of the 16th-century enrolments is Madeleine Gray, 'The Close Rolls as a source for sixteenth-century history', *Archives*, vol. xvii (1986), pp. 131-137.

[8a] See R. W. Ambler, 'Enrolled trust deeds – a source for the history of nineteenth-century nonconformity', *Archives*, 20 (1993), p. 177.

Class and Series		Comments and Indexes
Court of Chancery		
C53	Charter Rolls	Enrolments until *c*.1330. Published calendar.
C54	Close Rolls	Published calendar to 1509. Full indexes to grantees and grantors only; IND 9455-9457 (1,2) gives a list of people and places for 1558-66, and a list by county exists for 1680 onwards
J18	Enrolment Books	Continuation of C54 for 1903-1957
C66	Patent Rolls	Enrolled copies of Letters Patent, including Licenses to Alienate. See p.78
Court of Common Pleas		
CP40	Plea Rolls and from 1582 to 1833	(also known as De Banco Rolls) Listed Ed. I-18 Ed. II; IND 17174, 17168 for Ed. IV-Hen. VII; List 1539-1629 (indexed 1555-1629); IND 16944-16949 is a list (not indexed) for 1630-1836
CP43	Recovery Rolls	1583-1834
Exchequer		
E13	Exchequer of Plea Rolls	Selective list by place and party 1229-1820, including deeds with other local material. The principle of selection and the proportion of deeds covered is unclear.
E159	Queen's Remembrancer Memoranda Rolls	Indexed 1-35 Ed. I; otherwise, IND indexes year by year only, without summary indexes
E315	Augmentation Office Miscellaneous Books	Vols 209-247 (most) contain enrolments of Crown leases; some indexes
E368	LTR Memoranda Rolls	Similar to E159
Court of King's Bench		
KB26	Curia Regis Rolls continued after 1272 as	Calendar and index to 1242
KB27	Coram Rege Rolls continued after 1702 as	Indexed 1272-1326. Generally IND lists year by year. IND 1385-7 cover 1595-1649 (list of parties only)
KB122	Judgement Rolls	List of parties 1656-1805
Miscellaneous		
JUST1	Eyre Rolls	Contains a handful of early enrolments. No list or index.
E372	Pipe Rolls	Before 1195, these contain frequent enrolments. See *Pipe Roll Soc.*, passim
C52	Cartae Antiquae	1106 charters on 46 rolls (Rich. I-ED. II), mostly royal charters to monasteries, apparently continuing the practice of enrolment on the Pipe Rolls. Calendar, partly published (rolls 1-10) in I. Landon, *Pipe Roll Soc.* NS17 (1939)
CHES29	Plea Rolls	For Palatinate of Chester; continues as CHES30; partial calendar
CHES32	Enrolments	For Palatinate of Chester
DURH13	Judgement Rolls	For Palatinate of Durham
PL2	Close Rolls	For Palatinate of Lancaster; calendared
PL15	Plea Rolls	For Palatinate of Lancaster
[WALE16-26	Welsh Plea Rolls	Now in National Library of Wales]

Table 4 Deeds enrolled in the Royal Courts.

undertaken in the foreseeable future. With the available indexes, it is possible to follow the acquisitions by a person of fairly high social status as he built up a landed estate, or his declining fortunes as he sold land, but topographical study is virtually impossible. Occasionally, a private deed, say for the sale of a small part of a larger property, refers to the previous purchase of the whole property having been enrolled in Chancery, or on the Close Rolls, and these references can be located from the name of the original purchaser. Otherwise, the only possibility is a speculative and usually unsuccessful search for the name of someone who might have bought or sold land in a place of interest.

PRIVATE COPIES

Individuals and corporate bodies also attempted to safeguard their title deeds by making copies, particularly in the medieval period. The resulting volumes, known as cartularies, are a major source for medieval deeds, and something like 1,300 have survived. Most are no longer to be found with the deeds and other records with which they once belonged, and the best way to locate them is from G. R. C. Davis, *Medieval cartularies of Great Britain: a short catalogue* (London, 1958). The great majority of cartularies were produced by monasteries, and they are listed by Davis according to the monastic house concerned, followed by the few lay cartularies. There is no overall index of places covered, so the easiest way to discover possible cartulary evidence is by identifying former monastic owners. Davis's catalogue stops in 1535, and so omits the occasional later cartularies (for example the fine 'Grenville evidences' for Wootton Underwood, Buckinghamshire, now in the Henry E. Huntington Library, San Marino, California); however, these later examples are more likely still to be associated with their estate archives.

DISPERSED DEEDS

All the deeds described so far have come to rest in safe keeping and are accessible, even if their indexes are not as complete as would be wished. Sad to say, some deeds are suffering much worse fates, being sold as collections, or as single documents, or even being destroyed. It seems that most of the dispersed material originates in solicitors' offices. Despite attempts by the Law Society and the British Records Association to educate them, some solicitors are still throwing away the unwanted contents of their strong-rooms or giving dealers the chance to 'sort' through them. The result is that deed bundles are broken up, the unsaleable but historically vital abstracts of title and other papers destroyed, and the deeds taken off for sale. All this is clearly a breach of their professional responsibility, because the deeds do not belong to solicitors, but are in their possession for safe keeping. Furthermore, every archivist in the country will collect the unwanted material and keep it safely, while it remains formally the property of the depositor.

A particular danger time for deeds comes when ownership is first recorded at the Land Registry. At that moment, the old deeds are legally of no value. Even so, conservative solicitors tend to retain them in the deed bundle. Happily, others arrange for the deeds to reach the local record office, but sometimes they are thrown away or sold.

Building societies (and also banks) in their capacity as granters of mortgages hold immense numbers of deed bundles, almost always for properties which are recorded at the Land Registry. The majority of these bundles no doubt include only modern deeds, but a substantial minority certainly contain early ones as well. The problem posed for the societies by the bulk of their deed bundles is understandable but it has regrettably become clear that some building societies have recently shown an extremely irresponsible reaction. They have refused to accept the old deeds in the bundles, and have indicated to the solicitors concerned that they should be thrown away.[9] As the deeds are technically under the building societies' control, it would certainly be possible for them to combine their refusal with a strong recommendation, or even a requirement, that the old deeds are deposited at the local record office.

Some deeds come on to the market in substantial collections through the major sale rooms and antiquarian booksellers.[10] These probably eventually reach libraries (though not always accessible ones). Others are sold as single documents for a few pounds each through small booksellers, antique markets, or even—as I have seen—a shop at Disneyland in California. Thankfully, the fashion for parchment lamp-shades has passed, but despite this, with the deeds scattered among innumerable owners, they are lost as far as historical study is concerned. We can only hope that eventually they may be passed on to record offices or libraries. The absence of an individual deed may be regarded as unimportant, because of the overlap of information between one deed and another, though most deeds do provide some unique facts. Unfortunately, the dispersed material does not originate as isolated deeds, but as collections and deed bundles, whose sale from a stall in the Portobello Road does serious damage to the historical evidence available for the particular place concerned. There seems little chance of completely halting the trade in old deeds, though perhaps public-spirited individuals might be able to rescue some for record offices. The best hope may be to stop the trade at source, by persuading solicitors and owners to treat the material in their possession more responsibly.

As well as the scattered deeds that eventually reach collections in this country, a considerable number are now in North America (and a few in Australasia). Finding any of these that relate to particular places of interest is even more difficult than locating out-county material in British collections. Three or four United States libraries have acquired major estate archives more or less intact, and obviously they are essential sources for places belonging to the estates. The most important is the Henry E. Huntington Library, San Marino, California, whose biggest collection is the archive of the Dukes of Buckingham (Stowe, Buckinghamshire and many other places); they also have the Ellesmere (Cheshire) records, and medieval documents from Battle Abbey, Sussex, as well as a number of smaller collections. All these are well-described in the *Guide to British Historical Manuscripts in the Huntington Library* (Huntington Library, 1982), which includes an index of the places most frequently

---

[9] I have been told of this practice by solicitors on several occasions. See also a note in the magazine *Traditional Homes*, April 1986, p.4.

[10] The National Register of Archives scans sale catalogues from many of these sources and alerts county record offices to items of interest. Unfortunately, they do not also index the listed items by place or person, so that any items which are not acquired by record offices vanish again.

mentioned. The Joseph Regenstein Library, University of Chicago, holds the Bacon family archive (with a good unpublished catalogue). The archives of the North family of Kirtling, Cambridgeshire, have been acquired by the Kenneth Spencer Library, University of Kansas, Lawrence, Kansas (a detailed list is slowly being prepared). Finally, the Folger Shakespeare Library, Washington, D.C., has the estate collections of Paget of Blithfield and Ferrers of Tamworth (both from Staffordshire);[11] its smaller groups and numerous individual deeds are included in the published catalogue, but the major collections have separate lists (unpublished).

Unfortunately, as well as these reasonably well-known archives, a considerable number of other American university and public libraries own deeds, in numbers ranging from tens of thousands down to handfuls; I know of more than thirty such collections. Without exception they are unloved, poorly catalogued if at all, and in particular not listed by the National Register of Archives. Those that I have examined are rather mixed in character, and are clearly artificial collections, but they tend to emphasise a few places, for which they may be of great significance. Thus, Harvard Law Library includes what are recognisably the medieval deeds for Worth in Washfield Parish, Devon, whose later deeds are in the Devon Record Office. Happily, what was the largest group, the Wakefield collection at the Library of Congress, Washington D.C. (including about 1,000 deeds relating to Rothersfield, Hampshire and the estates of the Tylney family) has now been returned to the UK and the documents distributed to the relevant record offices; however, it may be some time before all these groups are catalogued and fully accessible, and the Library does still retain a small number of miscellaneous deeds obtained from other sources.[11a]

DEED CATALOGUES

An indication that the dispersal and sale of deeds is not exclusively a modern problem comes from a substantial number of catalogues of deeds for sale that were printed in the early years of the 20th century. Three main groups are known to me: the Coleman, Marcham and Moulton catalogues.[12] Even though the information they provide about each document is very sparse, they can be useful; the Marcham catalogue gives the only clue to the builder in 1671 of an unusual Buckinghamshire farmhouse.[13] Copies of these catalogues can be found in various libraries, and the Society of Genealogists has all of them, and also holds a slip index of personal names (but not places) in the Coleman catalogues. Some of the deeds listed in these catalogues may now be in libraries or record offices (for example, most of the Warwickshire deeds from Moulton's catalogue are in Birmingham Reference Library), but, for the majority, the catalogue remains the only evidence.

[11] See N.W. Alcock, 'The Ferrers of Tamworth Collection: Sorting and Listing', *Archives*, vol.19 (1991), pp.358-63.
[11a] For a brief description with a summary of the most important places represented, see N.W. Alcock, 'English Archives at the Library of Congress, Washington D.C.', *Archives*, 16 (1984), p. 273.
[12] J. Coleman, *Sale Catalogues of Deeds, etc.*, (265 catalogues, 1860-1913); F. Marcham, *The Antiquaries List of Deeds for Berkshire;* same for *Buckinghamshire, Middlesex* and *Surrey* (4 vols, *c.*1909); H.R. Moulton, *Palaeography, Genealogy and Topography*, 1930. I thank B.W. Christmas for reminding me of the significance of these sources, which were omitted from the first edition.
[13] Cowcroft, Latimer, Bucks; see N.W. Alcock, 'From Palladio to Potters Bar' in N. Burton (ed.), *Georgian Vernacular*, Georgian Group, 1995.

DEEDS IN PRIVATE HANDS

All the deeds so far described have become detached from the properties to which they relate, but of course deeds also exist in the 'right' place. Legally, it is only necessary for title deeds to prove ownership for 15 years, while most property ownership relies on Land Registry certificates. Despite this, many deed bundles include old deeds, usually extending into the 19th century, and quite often to the 18th or sometimes the 17th centuries. On one astounding occasion, I was shown the deeds of a west Devon farm which included a mid-14th-century charter, though I was not quite sure if it related to the farm itself, rather than to other property which had once belonged to the same family.

Private deeds can obviously be very useful, but tracking them down and obtaining permission to inspect them may be an onerous task. It is probably not advisable to undertake this systematically until the publicly-accessible sources have been checked. Naturally, if the local record office contains a long run of deeds identifiable as referring to a particular house or farm, then its later deeds may well not add much (though from the mid-19th century onwards, they may include plans). When part of a big estate was sold, it was very rare for any earlier deeds to be passed on. Any that survive are almost certainly among the estate records, which may or may not be in a record office.

Many people will want to start with the deeds of their own house, and this should be easy. Often, of course, a bank or building society has the deeds, but they will produce them for examination. The procedure for other private property is essentially the same, beginning naturally with a tactful request to the owner; he may well need to provide a written authorisation. Commercial property may pose more problems, starting with that of identifying the owner, as opposed to the occupier. However, by polite enquiry coupled with formal application by letter (emphasising that it is only the historical evidence of the old deeds that is of interest), I have been given access to deeds by a considerable number of organisations and firms (and I should here express my gratitude to them all).

Some corporate bodies own very large amounts of property. Almost all the Oxford and Cambridge colleges have their own muniment rooms, with their deeds reasonably well organised, including many relating to property they have sold. Breweries hold vast numbers of deeds for public houses, generally in regional offices. Some have made extensive deposits in local record offices (for example Watney-Mann in Norwich, Trowbridge, the Greater London Record Office, and elsewhere). It is to be hoped that this commendable practice will be adopted by other businesses. The major banks have their own archive offices in London, and their archivists generally have the deeds for the banks' own premises in their care, together with the occasional ownerless deed bundle that has come to light in their vaults. City, district and county councils own remarkable quantities of property, acquired especially through urban redevelopment and housing. Sometimes some of the early deeds have been passed on to local record offices, but in my experience they still hold much important historical material. They generally have large-scale maps showing what they own. The Government in the form of its various ministries has also acquired property for motorways, airfields and other defence installations, hospitals, etc. Some of the related deeds have reached the Public Record Office (and more may do so in the future), while some are held locally, but most are in the keeping of the Treasury Solicitor; in principle it is possible to obtain permission to inspect the deeds for particular properties for historical purposes.

Railtrack own much property, almost all acquired more than a century ago, whose deeds should be of great interest. This applies particularly to urban areas where they were likely to buy complete properties. For their rural land, large deed bundles are much less likely, because they normally bought strips of land forming parts of larger properties, and received only abstracts of the earlier deeds. Occasionally their deeds have reached local record offices by accident (e.g. those for the Leamington to Rugby branch of the London and North-Western Railway in Warwick Record Office), but most are held at their head office. The only ones I have inspected (for a small part of the former London and Birmingham Railway) were rather disappointing in that they had been weeded of almost everything except the purchase deeds themselves, but in other regions the bundles are apparently much more complete.

One point should be re-emphasised: especially when examining any private deeds, it is essential to make one's notes as detailed as possible, even noting material that does not seem directly relevant, such as other property included in the deeds. It is clearly unreasonable to expect owners to permit access to the same documents time after time.

ON THE TRAIL

With good luck, private deed bundles will give good runs, perhaps back into the 18th century, but if not, the situation may not be hopeless. One of the principal reasons for the absence of early deeds is that they were not passed on to a purchaser because they were relevant to other property belonging to the seller. If so, the sale deed is likely to include an agreement ('covenant') to produce the previous deeds. A covenant of a date much earlier than 1900 is probably not worth pursuing; one must hope that the old deeds come to light in one of the places already discussed. With a 20th-century sale, the chance of successfully following up such a lead is very much better. It should be noted that, although the covenant to produce previous deeds is in principle legally enforceable, strictly speaking this only applies to the original seller and purchaser. In any case, the most interesting deeds will be the earliest, probably preceding any included in the covenant. However, the main problem is not getting permission to look at the deeds, but locating them. If the property belonged to an estate which is still a going concern, then the deeds can reasonably be expected to be either in a local record office, or still with the estate. Often though, the seller or his descendants cannot be identified. Usually the existing deed bundle contains an Abstract of Title (very important documents, discussed in detail on p.57), and this is invaluable for making further progress, as well as giving a summary of the previous ownership. The abstract generally carries on the cover the name of the solicitor who prepared it, and he is likely either to have the deeds, or to be able to locate them. If the name is not on the cover, then it can almost certainly be found in the handwritten notes made on the abstract by the purchaser's solicitor, when checking the correctness of the abstract. These take the form 'Examined with the original at the offices of … (solicitor's name and address) … (date)'.

A success story about a small farmhouse in the Breconshire hills illustrates what can be achieved. The first original title deed was no earlier than 1967, when the house was sold off from the farmland. The abstract of title only went back to a sale in 1945 following the death of the then owner, and attempts to follow up his relatives achieved nothing. Progress came through the help of the owner of the farm's land. His deeds went no further back, but did include one vital document, the abstract of title for the 1945 sale. This started with a will of 1875, which set up an elaborate family trust, eventually wound up in 1935. It also gave the name of the Brecon solicitors who had produced the deeds for inspection. Inquiry from them revealed that they held a bundle of documents which included not only the deeds from 1875 to 1935 but also those back to 1786, with a recital of one of 1759. So, with several people's assistance, a solid 200 years of the farm's history were documented.

NEW WAYS TO FIND DEEDS[14]

Some of the vast quantity of information accessible via the World Wide Web is becoming useful for locating original deeds and other records of value to local and family historians, and much more is promised for the future. The most important resources already available are probably the manuscript catalogue of the British Library and the PRO on-line catalogue. Both of these directly identify individual people and places, though they only provide indexes to descriptions in their own sometimes eccentric spelling; this is a particular problem with texts taken from the PRO Catalogues of Ancient Deeds, for which several alternative spellings may need to be tried. Several county and other record offices now have searchable lists, and some of these include personal and place indexes rather than just searchable descriptions. These sites include Essex, Surrey and Gwynedd Record Offices, the Universities of Hull (its complete collection, mainly relating to the East Riding of Yorkshire), and Nottingham (some collections) and the 1,000 deeds at Harvard Law Library.[15] A major advance should come within the next couple of years from the time of writing (2001), through the Access to Archives (A2A) initiative being coordinated by the Public Record Office. Its target is to place up to half a million pages of record office catalogues on the web, much of it relating to family and estate collections.

All these existing and prospective sources should have personal and place indexes, but it is not yet obvious that these will be easy to use for local and family history as opposed to thematic studies; it is also not clear whether the A2A indexes will be over-arching or whether each source will have to be searched separately. An ideal on-line index for people or places should be structured and browsable, so that groups of similar names appear together, while the corresponding lists should appear on screen at the same time (e.g. in an adjoining frame), so that they can also be browsed; place names should (optionally) be grouped by county, to bring together items likely to be relevant to each other. It should also be possible to move forward and back in the calendars themselves from a particular point located through the indexes, to examine the inter-relationship between individual documents.

---

[14] Web addresses are listed on p. 119.
[15] Also including an on-line exhibition of 150 items with informative descriptions: http://www.law.harvard.edu/library/special/exhibitions/history_in_deed/index.htm.

4
How?

This chapter explains how to recognise the important types of deed, and how to extract their significance from their legal jargon. The links between the various types are examined, but the purely legal aspects of how conveyancing was undertaken and how it has changed through the centuries are not over-emphasised, as this is relatively unimportant for the historical application of deed evidence. Instead of quoting a series of complete deeds as examples, the key sections of individual deeds are examined separately. This is intended to make it easier for the reader to match the content of the deeds he is studying with the examples described. However, typical complete texts are included in Appendix I.

A major division in the comparative difficulty of understanding deeds comes at the very end of the medieval period (around 1550). This corresponds to the change from deeds mainly in Latin to those mainly in English, to an improvement in the legibility of handwriting (helpful to those without palaeographic expertise), and to changes in the types of deeds used (and also in their size). The chapter is therefore split between post-medieval deeds (in English with minor exceptions), and medieval deeds (in Latin). A third section deals briefly with various documents which are not title deeds proper but either are often found in deed bundles or are related to deeds, and a fourth with property transactions in manor courts. A detailed discussion of palaeography is not included, but some aids are listed under Further Information (p.117). Most deeds are fairly easy to read from about 1700 onwards and, before then, they tend to be very much better written than, say, letters or informal accounts. However, even 18th- and early 19th-century deeds may have occasional words that can only be deciphered with great difficulty, by much comparison with the same (or perhaps different) letters in words that can be recognised; this arises because of the very stylised letter forms used by the lawyers' clerks. It can be rather easy to misread names, unless particular care is taken, and even 19th-century abstracters made mistakes on occasion. As a help for this period, a page of letter forms is given in Appendix III.

TENURE

An important idea for understanding the meaning of deeds (especially medieval ones) is that of *tenure*, that one person holds property from someone else. In legal principle, all land in England belonged to the king (by right of conquest by William I) and everyone except him held their land from someone else. The king granted it to his nobles to hold of him as his tenants. They in turn granted manors to their retainers to hold by knight service (sending knights to fight when required). Finally,

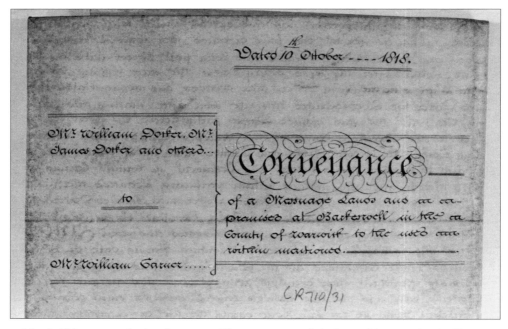

14 A 19th-century deed endorsement. These are a great help in working out the significance of a deed. [WRO CR710/31]

the various inhabitants of the manor held of its lord, paying a money rent or doing work on his land.

By the post-medieval period, we can recognise three main types of tenure: *freehold*, property held freely and for ever (effectively ownership as we know it now), *leasehold*, property held by a lease for a given period from a freeholder, and *copyhold*, property held as part of a manor, whose ownership was recognised by a copy of an entry on the manor court roll. Other forms of tenure/ownership, e.g. burgage tenure, tenure in free socage, ceased to have any substantial legal significance in the post-medieval period.

POST–MEDIEVAL DEEDS
INTRODUCTION

ENDORSEMENTS

Even before a deed is unfolded, the writing on the outside (the endorsement) may explain what it is. In the 19th century it was standard practice to write an identifying endorsement when the deed was drawn up (Illus.14). This gives the date, the type of deed, the two principal people involved (sometimes saving much effort identifying them among half-a-dozen or more in the deed itself), and the property involved. However, the deed itself should always be looked at as well, because it gives much more information on all these aspects.

15 Seventeenth-century deed endorsements. The main endorsement, 'The deed of the house I bought of the Citty in Greefryer Lane' (Coventry), is typical of the period, as is the 18th-century note, '14 Sept 1617 Feoffment from Mayor etc. of Coventry to Basnett for £20'. However, the two 'secret endorsements' are unique. The initial impression is 'Double Dutch', though the code is not difficult to break, merely involving writing the initial letter of each word at the end. The combination of the code and some eccentric spelling makes the text unusually difficult to transcribe, but my best reading is: (i) het ortyf ivef oundp hatt Mr ristpherC wenO adh intw uto het 15 fo eauboaryF ni 1658; (ii) Mr asnitB asw aydp ish onym orf het tabells yb eem & aanJ ochr pu ni Mr romellsb hamberc ulyJ 19 1667. [WRO CR457/Coventry]

Original endorsements of this sort were not a normal 17th- or 18th-century practice (with a few exceptions, such as leases granted by major estates). However, the majority of deeds of this period have been endorsed, usually somewhat later than they were written. Series of numbers are common, indicating the order of deeds in the bundle, which are helpful in showing whether any have been lost. They are often accompanied by a brief note of the date and subject (Illus.15). More exotic endorsements are sometimes found, though rarely as bizarre as the secret writing on the example illustrated. An endorsement reading 'examined and produced in the case of A v. B' is particularly significant; it indicates that the deed was used as evidence in a lawsuit. From the date and the names of the participants, it should be possible to find further records of the case.[1]

---

[1] Finding this in the Public Record Office may be tedious, involving, for example, working through lists for each of the 'Six Clerks' of the Court of Chancery. However, success can be rewarded by very interesting information. A useful guide to the sources for tracing particular cases is Henry Horowitz, *Chancery Equity Records and Proceedings, 1600-1800: a guide to the documents in the Public Record Office* (H.M.S.O., 1996).

Endorsements are particularly useful when starting on a bundle of deeds. It is generally best to work in chronological order, as later deeds often repeat the information of earlier ones, but without all the details; thus, if an earlier deed has been covered, a later one can be dealt with quickly; exceptionally, if the latest deeds give a clear modern description of the property (e.g. with its street number), it may be useful to start with this. The first step will probably be to skim through the bundle and check the endorsements and dates, only opening those deeds without dates on the outside. Even though most deed bundles are out of order, the actual order of the documents should never be altered without permission from the record office staff, because this order may convey 'invisible' information which, once lost, can never be regained (see Illus.2). It is also worth remembering that the precise chronological order may not be the most informative. For example, if a bundle contains deeds for two properties which were later combined, the earlier deeds belong in two distinct sequences.

When the deed is unfolded, the dorse (back) often carries other text, not connected with the endorsements which identify it. Most of this is formal, and virtually repeats information more easily found in the deed itself. The dorse also has the signatures of the witnesses to the deed. In contrast to the medieval period (see p.91), these were usually lawyer's clerks, and the names are of little importance (but for an exception, see p.79). Receipts for purchase money or mortgage repayments may also be recorded. Occasionally, endorsements are significant, and include such things as schedules of furniture, lists of debts, or of strips in open fields. More often, such details are on extra sheets of parchment attached to the bottom of the deed. These schedules are sometimes extremely interesting as, for example, in two deeds for the manor of Faccombe, Hampshire; the first of these (1583) attaches 'a pedigree ... from whome the landes ... did descende', chattily reciting the complicated ownership of the manor; the second (1634) lists room by room the goods that were to be removed by the owner when he passed the manor on to his son (University of Kansas, Kenneth Spenser Library, HF7:160, 154).

Finally, especially in the 19th century, one may find a complete second deed, or references to one, written on the back of the original at a later date. These are likely to be either the reconveyance of a mortgage (its cancellation after repayment); or a note that part of the property has been sold, possibly with a record of the agreement to produce the deed on request to some other interested party (e.g. the purchaser).

DATING

The only major problem with dating post-medieval deeds comes from the practice of starting the year on 25 March, which was in use before 1752 ('Old Style', as opposed to 'New Style'). Without overwhelming evidence to the contrary, any date from 1 January to 24 March can be assumed to belong to the next calendar year, e.g. 17 February 1724 is really 1725. This should be recorded as 1724[/5], using square brackets because this is your inference; sometimes original documents follow this style, and then your transcript can show 1724/5 without brackets. If there is any doubt, the date can be checked from the alternative method used in deeds, dating by regnal year. For example, consider the case of '10 February in the second year of King George the First'. George I came to the throne in 1714, but this date is 1716, because the day of his accession was 1 August. It is not difficult to work out the year from a list of the accession dates of the sovereigns, but much the easiest way is to consult the excellent tables in C.R. Cheney's *Handbook of Dates* (Cambridge, 2000). Indeed this book is so useful that anyone working with deeds should probably buy their own, so that precious record office time can be saved for looking at documents.

Both year and regnal date are given in deeds from the Restoration until about 1840, but before 1650 the year is less common (sometimes included at the very end of the deed). The convenience of including the year probably became clear during the Commonwealth, when deeds were dated 'In the year of our Lord God, according to the computation of the Church of England'. Curiously, the only omission from the *Handbook of Dates* is a table covering the Commonwealth period, and showing the dates of Easter, Calendar Table, etc. This is provided in Table 5.

Year	Regnal year of Charles II*	Easter Day	Calendar Table in Handbook of Dates
1650	1,2	14 April	24
1651	2,3	30 March	9
1652	3,4	18 April	28
1653	4,5	10 April	20
1654	5,6	26 March	5
1655	6,7	15 April	25
1656	7,8	6 April	16
1657	8,9	29 March	8
1658	9,10	11 April	21
1659	10,11	3 April	13

* Charles II counted his reign as starting from the day his father was beheaded (30 January 1649), though I have never encountered deeds dated by his regnal years before his Restoration in 1660.

Table 5 Calendar Table for the Commonwealth period.

SHAPES AND PATTERNS

Most post-medieval deeds share a common physical shape, with an indented (wavy) top, and are therefore generally called 'indentures' and start 'This indenture'. In theory this implies that, as in the medieval period, two copies were made, one for each party, that could be fitted together (see p. 84), but in practice most deeds had only one copy and when more were made (e.g. for a lease and counterpart), they do not fit together; there are also often many more than two parties, but not all would receive copies of the deed. It is also convenient to know that when a multi-page deed is unfolded, the first (indented) sheet is at the bottom and the last sheet with the signatures is on top. By the 19th century, indentures were of a standard size with sheets of parchment measuring 33 by 25 ins. (85 by 65 cms.), folded up to 11 by 9 ins. (28 by 23 cms.).

Form	Initial phrase	Shape	Illus./page	Comment
Indenture	This Indenture	Rectangle with top edge indented, as it involves two parties. Can have many sheets	17 p.62	The most important form
Feoffment	*Sciant presentes* Know all men	Rectangle. Not indented, as it is a declaration by one party		Survival of medieval form
Quitclaim	To all Christian people	As feoffment		As feoffment (commoner)
Fine	*Hec est finalis concordia* (English after 1733). This is the final concord	Long rectangle, two edges indented	20 p.74	Specialised handwriting
Bond	*Noverint Universi per presentes me* (after 1733) Know all men by these presents. The condition of this obligation …	Upright rectangle, two sections, first Latin later English (often printed), second section English (second section)	19 p.71	
Recovery	George by the Grace of God …	Rectangle with suspended seal (often in tin box)	21 p.76	Specialised and difficult handwriting
Letters Patent	Elizabeth by the Grace of God …	Rectangle, ornamented with royal portrait, suspended Great Seal	22 p.78	
Copy of Court Roll	Name of Place View of Frankpledge, or Court Baron	Rectangle, two paragraphs, sometimes in Latin	25 p.96	

Table 6 Types of post-medieval deeds.

Some other forms of deed are found, which can usually be recognised from their appearance and their initial phrases. Most of these are not indented, because ostensibly they were declarations by one person rather than agreements between two. They are summarised in Table 6.

Indentures follow a standard pattern in their text as well as their shape. Each consists of one monstrous sentence, followed by a second short sentence witnessing the first. This first sentence is always made up of a number of sections or clauses dealing with different aspects, arranged in broadly the same order. It is essential to be able to recognise these clauses in order to identify the various types of indenture and to extract their historical evidence.

The different clauses are described in Table 7. Not all occur in every deed, while some may be repeated. Each usually starts with a characteristic phrase, that is his

This Indenture made the   day of

in the year of our Lord one thoufand feven hundred and ninety   and in the   year of the

reign of our Sovereign Lord George the   of Great Britain France and Ireland King Defender

of the Faith and fo forth **Between**

of the one part and

of the other part

Witneffeth that for and in Confideration of the Sum of five fhillings of lawful money

of Great Britain to the faid   in hand paid by the faid

at or before the fealing and delivery of thefe Prefents the

Receipt whereof is hereby acknowledged and for other good Caufes and Confiderations the faid

hereunto moving He the faid

Hath Bargained and Sold and by thefe Prefents **Doth** Bargain and Sell unto the faid

h   Executors Adminiftrators and Affigns **All**

16   Printed blank deed form dating from the 1790s, one of a variety of examples from an old-established solicitor's files. From the start of a mortgage by Lease and Release in 16 printed sheets (original size 28 by 38 cm) (WRO CR1596/box 91).

sometimes written in capitals or otherwise emphasised. These phrases are so standard, that it was even possible for them to be printed, leaving blanks for the significant text to be written in (Illus.16).[2]

The differences between the various clauses in different types of deeds are the main concern of the following sections. A little practice, coupled with a knowl-edge of the standard pattern, makes the study of deeds very much more rapid than might seem possible at first. For example, you come to a pair of deeds (a lease and release) in the middle of a sequence of deeds, identified on the outside as a

[2]   Although this collection contains a considerable number of these forms, I have never seen one used for an actual deed. It may be that they were intended for producing drafts of deeds, that were then copied onto parchment for signature.

The texts are usually more repetitive than shown here, e.g. for the action clause of a Release, 'hath, granted, bargained, sold, released, and confirmed, and doth grant, bargain, sell, release and confirm'.

Clause	Text	Comments and Significance
Introduction	**This Indenture** tripartite	Bipartite (2), quadripartite, etc., depending on the number of parties
Date	**dated the**	
Parties	**Between ... of the first part and ... of the second part,** etc. **Witnesseth that**	The people concerned. One party may consist of several people
Recital	**Whereas ...**	Describes previous transactions, sometimes very numerous
	Now the said ...	'Now' ends the recital
Consideration	**for and in consideration of ...**	Often the actual sum of money; sometimes a cautious 'for good and sufficient consideration', or 'for natural love and affection'; 5s. for minor parties. The end of the recital may explain how the consideration was to be paid.
Action	**doth demise** (lease) or **grant** or **release** or **assign ... unto ...**	These are the main alternatives though each is wrapped up in many more words
Property	**All that messuage ... together with all ways watercourses, ...**	The property involved. Such inclusive clauses do not mean that the property included any watercourses, etc., but guard against any omissions
	(and also ...)	Another property, or something like a right of way
	together with all title deeds ...	Alternatively 'such deeds as relate solely' to the property
	To have and to hold the said messuage ... to the said ... his heirs and assigns ...	
Period	**For the term of ...** (or) **For ever**	An important distinction between a permanent grant and one for a limited period, long or short
Tenure	**To be holden of the chief lord ...**	Not always included. A medieval survival that can be ignored
Rent	**Yielding and paying ...**	The rent, if any
Uses	**to the use of the said ...**	Who benefits—this clause can be very complex
Conditions and Covenants	**Subject to ...** **and the said ...** **further covenanteth ...**	By far the most variable clause with both formal and significant covenants
Warranty	**And the said ... warranteth that he hath not done any action ...**	A restatement of the right of the seller to the property
Witness	**In witness whereof the said ... hath hereunto set his name and seal the day and year above written**	
Seals and Signatures		Applied to the binding fold. Post-medieval seals normally have little significance
Dorse		Carries the witnesses to the signing, sometimes with receipts and additional memoranda

Table 7 Clauses of post-medieval indentures.

conveyance by A and mortgagees to B. First, the small lease is passed over, and probably need not even be opened. In the release, the parties are examined, and consist of A, who has been seen before, though now his abode has changed from the local town to a nearby village; his mortgagees as named in an earlier mortgage deed (already examined); and B and his dower trustee (see p.63), who are new and must be recorded in full. 'Whereas' introduces a long recital of the mortgage which is skipped through as it repeats the earlier deed. On the last page, 'Now' is immediately followed by the consideration, which is new information, and the property, which is the same as before, except that B is named as the occupier. A glance over the covenants and conditions shows only formal clauses, except that a lease to B made two years earlier is excepted from the conveyance, because still current; even though B is apparently the beneficiary, he might have assigned it to a third person. This lease is not in the bundle and so a final note is made. In a total time of less than five minutes, all the unique information has been gleaned. Of course if this is the earliest deed in the bundle, and it has no abstract of title for earlier ones, a careful summary would need to be made of the recitals and the property because these are new and not repeated.

It is often convenient to record the evidence of a deed on a standard form, and a possible layout is included in Appendix II. This can be particularly useful if the type of deed is not immediately clear, as much of the form can be filled in before the deed is completely understood. Also, if the logical order of the deeds is uncertain, the forms can be shuffled. It is possible to use file cards for individual deeds, but unfortunately a standard five by three-inch card is really too small for most deeds. With experience, and with a well-ordered deed bundle, an alternative to either forms or cards is to record the deeds in the same way as on an abstract of title (next section). This involves listing for each deed the date on the left, and the details on the right, following on one after another.

The primary analysis of a deed bundle should not depend on whether it is for local or family history. The local historian needs all the information on property and its changes, but must also keep a watch on the people involved. The family historian's concern with people should not cause him to ignore the property, for which in due course he may want all the details available to help him locate it and understand its significance for his ancestors' social standing and financial dealings.

ABSTRACTS OF TITLE

In principle, every bundle of title deeds should contain one or more abstracts of title, covering all the deeds and possibly running back before the first original. In practice, lawyers' clerks seem to have thrown out old abstracts, so that it is common to find deeds without abstracts even in coherent bundles, while when the deeds have been scattered, the abstracts have almost always vanished. Naturally, when an abstract describes deeds that are not in the bundle, notes should be taken with the utmost care, because it contains evidence that may now exist nowhere else at all. A good example

Type	Page	Clause	Nature
Lease	59	Action	Demise, set and to farm let
		Period	Various, e.g. 21 years; life; three lives
		Rent	Full market rent or small reserved rent
Lease & Release	61	Consideration	5s
(i) Lease for year		Action	Bargain and sell (usually)
		Period	Year (sometimes 6 months)
		Rent	Peppercorn
(ii) Release	63	Action	Hath granted, bargained and sold … being in his actual possession
		Period	For ever
Mortgage	68	Action	Grant, bargain and sell and demise
		Period	500 or 1,000 years (usually)
		Rent	Peppercorn
Assignment of Mortgage	69	Action	Assign and set over
Assignment to attend inheritance	70	Uses	To B in trust for A, to wait upon and attend the inheritance
Feoffment *and* Bargain and Sale	79	Action	Given, granted, alienated, bargained and sold and enfeoffed
		Endorsement	Feoffment: Livery of seizin; Bargain and Sale; Enrolment in court
Quitclaim	80	Action	Remise, release and for ever quitclaim

Table 8   Post-medieval indentures: Summary of principal clauses.

is that for Chapel Street, Warwick, described above (p.14), which includes details back to 1723 although the earliest deed is of 1819. As here, the abstract often covers about 100 years, which was considered a sufficient period to establish a secure title. When the deeds in the bundle are being examined, the abstract can save a lot of effort, but the aims of the abstractor should be borne in mind. His vital concern was to ensure that the seller (whose title to the property was described) was clearly the owner. Thus he paid great attention to the legal details of each deed to make sure it had the right form and included the right people. He was rather less concerned with the descriptions of property, particularly when the property of interest was only part of that in the deed, and he might omit the irrelevant sections with the comment *inter alia* (among other property). He might also simplify some of the personal details. Thus for historical purposes, an abstract of title makes an excellent route-map through a deed bundle and saves a lot of work, but if the deeds exist it is important to check their details against the abstract.

TYPES OF POST-MEDIEVAL DEED

The general pattern will now be described in detail for the different types of deed. If there is no convenient endorsement, it may not be at all clear at first what sort of deed is being looked at (and this applies just as much to 'experts' as to 'beginners'). Even if the deed does not follow a standard pattern, working through clause by clause will eventually locate the key phrases. These key phrases for the major types of deeds are summarised in Table 8. The most common deed types that do not follow the pattern are instantly recognisable, being the bond, fine, recovery, and copy of court roll (see Illus.19-21, 25 and p.94). Others are sufficiently straightforward that they can be easily identified, and their analysis should not need extra help (e.g. articles of agreement or building contracts). There remain a few more types of deeds or deed-like documents that are extremely rare. If you encounter one of these, then it is very reasonable to seek help from the archivist.

Lease and Counterpart Lease; Assignment of Lease

The lease makes a convenient point to start. It is a common and relatively straight-forward deed that usually means what it says, while its derivatives are involved in several other types (especially the lease and release and the perpetual leasehold, pp.61 and 81). Tenants of property such as small cottages often held 'at will', without any written lease, but for anything more substantial, two copies of the lease were prepared. One was signed by the owner and given to the tenant. This is the *lease* itself. The other was signed by the tenant and kept by the owner. This is the *counterpart lease* or *counterpart*. The distinction between the two can be useful in deciding where a particular document comes from, though if a lease was given up before it expired (was surrendered), the surrendered lease (sometimes endorsed to this effect) would be returned to the owner's archives. Alternatively, the tenant might assign his rights to someone else by an *assignment of lease*. He might also sub-let (under-lease) the prop-erty or part of it, though both assignments and sub-leasing were often controlled by conditions in the original lease (usually requiring the owner's permission). The main difference between the two is that with an assigned lease, the owner would receive his rent from the new tenant, but a sub-tenant paid the original tenant who then paid the owner. In 18th-century building development in towns such as Bath, whole nests of leases are found, with the property owner granting a 99-year lease of a block of land to a developer, the latter laying out plots and under-leasing to a builder, and the house when built being under-leased again to the tenant.

A *reversionary lease* or *lease in reversion* starts after some specified future event has taken place, e.g. the death of a life tenant or the expiry of a current lease, and the property has 'reverted' to the landlord.

The special features of a lease are as follows:

Parties: These are (1) the true owners or perhaps the trustees of a marriage or family settlement (which will be mentioned in a recital), and (2) the tenant who is usually, but not necessarily the occupier.

Consideration: A sum of money, an *entry fine*, was often paid for a lease, especially if the rent was a token one. The surrender of a previous lease may also be recorded here.

Action: The key words are 'demise, set and to farm let'.

Property: See below (p.65).

Period: This is either a term of years (14 and 21 being common, as is 99 years for building leases), or sometimes one year, to continue year by year until notice is given by either party (a yearly lease), or until some event takes place, e.g. during the life of the tenant (a life lease). A form of the latter particularly popular in south-west England, but not uncommon elsewhere, was the 'three-life lease', for 99 years or until the death of the last of three named people (all living when the lease was granted). For example, a lease of 1613 for Sowton, Devon, was for the lives of Thomas Pyne, his wife Agnes and their son, Leonard.[3] This made a very secure tenure for the farmer and his immediate family which could later be extended. We are told that for some farms this went on for centuries, so that only the owner and the farmer himself were aware that it was not a freehold.[4] In the 18th century, such leases were calculated by estate administrators as equivalent to 60-year terms; during this century they were gradually replaced by 21-year leases.[5] Three-life leases were also used in Ireland, where they caused considerable trouble in the 19th century, as the 'lives' emigrated and no-one knew whether they were alive or dead.

With three-life leases, reversions were often granted 'to add one life to two'. This lease started on the death of the two surviving lives, and so brought the number of people on whom the tenancy depended back to three. Alternatively, the surrender of the original lease might be part of the consideration for a new lease for three lives. This had exactly the same effect, unless the reversionary lease was granted to a different tenant, possibly even one who had outbid the original tenant for the renewal. The starting-date of a lease is always stated, and Lady Day (25 March) and Michaelmas (29 September) were usual.

Rent: This is a real sum, not a token (peppercorn) as in the lease for a year. It was usually paid in two parts, on Lady Day and Michaelmas. Some leases, especially those for 'three lives', had rather small rents, e.g. 6s. 8d., coupled with large entry fines. The fines might then vary from renewal to renewal of the lease, while the rent was constant. A 'rack rent' is occasionally referred to in a deed (though more often in rentals and estate documents). It has two very different meanings. Originally, it described a rent comprising a very high proportion of the holding's profit, the term being derived from the instrument of torture. Such a rent might be extorted if the landlord wanted the maximum immediate income, irrespective of the future decay of the property; thus, 19th-century Irish landlords frequently demanded them. However, generally speaking, in estate practice of the late 19th century the term had lost its pejorative flavour, and the rack rent merely represented the full market rental. This was often calculated by a rule of thumb allowing one-third of the holding's profit to the owner (as rent), one-third to the tenant (his living expenses), and one-third for the land (the return on the tenant's capital, used for purchase of stock, etc.).

Other payments and services are listed with the rent. These might include 'suit of court' (attendance at the manor court, usually twice a year) and 'heriot' (in three-life leases, a payment on the death of one of the intermediate lives). A rent of a cock or a hen at Christmas or Easter is not uncommon, and other rents in kind sometimes occur, e.g. '500 couples of conies [rabbits]', from the tenant of a warren or the 'two

---

[3] N.W. Alcock, 'Fields and Farms in an East Devon Parish', *Trans. Devonshire Ass.*, vol.107 (1975), p.93.

[4] A technical distinction was made between a simple life lease, which had no definite end, and a lease for three lives or 99 years. The former legally transferred the freehold and therefore by law needed to be conveyed as freehold, e.g. by feoffment. In reality, of course, the property leased for lives would revert to the original owner in due course.

[5] See R. Stanes, 'Conversion from Three-life leases to Leases for Years', in W. Minchinton (ed.), *Agricultural Improvement: Medieval and Modern* (University of Exeter, 1981).

Type	Comments
1. *Formal*	
Quiet enjoyment	The landlord will not prevent the tenant using the property
Maintenance	To maintain the buildings in good condition
Distraint or re-entry	Usually, if the rent was unpaid, the landlord could distrain after, say 21 days, i.e. collect goods to the value of the rent. After a year's arrears, the lease was void, and the landlord could re-enter. As most leases ran to completion without trouble, these clauses were rarely used
2. *Significant*	
Building	Tenant or landlord to build or rebuild a house or barn, etc. within a specified time. Usually with a detailed description of the new building
Carriage	E.g. to carry two cartloads of coal per year from Nuneaton to Stoneleigh Abbey, Warws. [SBT DR18/1/992; 1683]; may be part of the rent clause
Husbandry	E.g. a financial penalty on ploughing more than a specified part of the land within the last five years of the lease, or to apply specified amounts of manure or other fertilizer
Social	'to attend and bee ready with a nagge, horse or mare to ride with ... Henry Raynsford [*lord of the manor*] when he shall bee thereunto requested, the said Henry Hobbins [*tenant's son*] having his livery cloake or coate allowed unto him by the said Henry Raynsford' [SBT DR33/10; 1623].

Table 9 Conditions in post-medieval leases.

firkins of barrel butter all good, swete, merchantable and of the best, every firkin to waye threescore and foure poundes' to be delivered every year at Michaelmas [1611 lease of a farm in Hoo, Suffolk; University of Kansas, Kenneth Spenser Library, HF2:11].

Covenants and conditions: Conditions were frequently attached to leases. Some are formal, almost always present, rather obvious, and not very important. However, the end of a lease should always be checked for unusual conditions, and a few samples are given in Table 9.[6]

The structure of an **assignment of lease** is not very close to that of a lease, but as they are closely related in their function, the assignment is described here. Its significant clauses are:

Parties: The usual parties will be (1) the original tenant, (2) the new tenant, possibly with (3) the owner, if his permission was needed for the assignnment.

Recital: The grant of the original lease is always recited. Consideration: Something can be expected here.

Action: The key phrase is 'assign and set over'.

The remaining clauses will either be repeated from the original lease, or will be covered by phrases like 'as in the hereinbefore recited indenture ...'.

LEASE AND RELEASE

Unlike most other indentures, the two linked deeds which make up the Lease and Release do not perform a single function, but rather provide a form which was

---

[6] Covenants are further discussed with special reference to those concerning building work by K.T. Ward, 'Covenants in conveyancing instruments: a note for the vernacular architectural historian', *Vernacular Architecture*, vol.25 (1994), pp.16–19.

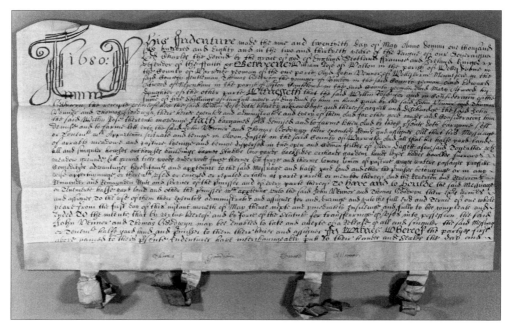

17 The lease of a lease and release. Although smaller than most post-medieval indentures, this shows their typical form. Its archival place is folded up inside the Release and in the 19th century it is sometimes physically attached to the bottom of the Release. For text see p.104. [WRO CR607/Coventry]

employed for many tasks. However, the form originated as a conveyance to transfer property from one person to another, and this function is described here. The lease and release was invented in about 1600 to provide a secret but legally valid conveyance. The first part of the lease and release is a lease of the property by the vendor to the purchaser for one year at a nominal rent (Illus.17). This puts the purchaser in possession as tenant. Then, on the following day, the vendor and anyone with an interest in the property release their rights to the purchaser, leaving him in full ownership. Because the release only transferred an *interest* in the property (the reversion after the expiry of the lease) rather than the freehold itself, it did not have to be made public by enrolment or livery of seizin (unlike the bargain and sale or feoffment; p.79). The lease and release gained popularity steadily during the 17th century until in the 18th and early 19th centuries it was virtually the only form of conveyance.[7] The lease part of the lease and release was no longer needed after 1841 with the passage of 'A Statute for rendering a Release as effectual for the conveyance of a freehold estate as a Lease and Release' (as it is sometimes referred to in deeds of the period). The Real Property Act of 1845 finally allowed freehold property to be conveyed by a single private deed.

---

[7]   The earliest example I have encountered is of 1633 (SBT, ER3/306-7), but D. Smith of Gloucester Record Office informs me that he has seen an example of 1530; there may have been some special reason for using the lease and release form in this early example.

The details by which the two parts of a lease and release can be recognised are as follows:

1. *Lease for a year*: (also called 'bargain and sale for a year')
Parties: These are usually the actual owner and the actual purchaser.
Consideration: Normally five shillings (useful for identification).
Action: Either 'demise' as for an ordinary lease or 'bargain and sell'.
Property: The full detail of the property is always given.
Period: One year (occasionally six months in the 17th century).
Rent: Usually 'a peppercorn if legally demanded'.
Uses: 'To the end and intent that ... the said B may be in actual possession'.

2. *Release*
Although releases may be fairly simple if the conveyance has no complications (as in the example on p.110), they can be very lengthy, particularly in the recital section. The extent to which this can be skipped depends on whether the deeds referred to have already been seen, or are described in an abstract of title. Because the release is the single most important type of title deed, this is the best point to examine the parties and the property (see p.65).
Parties: The simplest possibility is (1) the seller, (2) the purchaser, and this is common until the mid-18th century. Quite often the description of the seller includes his connection to a previous owner, e.g. 'John Clarke, son of Jeremiah Clarke, late of Ettington, deceased'. Joint owners were usually the result of a joint inheritance, but occasionally two people made a purchase as partners; such joint owners were generally 'tenants in common', implying that they owned a half share each, and their shares could be sold, left by will, etc. The alternative of 'joint tenants' or 'tenants in survivorship' meant that, if one purchaser died, the other automatically succeeded to both shares.

A very important distinction has to be made between straightforward ownership as just described, and the more complex situation in which the owners in the eyes of the law purchased or sold property on behalf of someone else. The latter was the 'beneficial' owner, who received the benefit of the property. Trustees make up the main group of these legal owners, and executors of a will are other examples; they were frequently instructed to sell the deceased's property, and they would then be the first party of the deed. Among trustees, apart from dower trustees (next paragraph), those of marriage or family settlements (p.72) are most common, but trustees in bankruptcy are also found. For all of these, the recital should explain their position, but it does not always make quite clear who was the previous owner.

For the purchaser, an important change took place in the later 18th century. Before this he acted straightforwardly as an individual, but thereafter he was usually associated with his own trustee, a dower trustee. The legal title to the property was held by the trustee, so that, on the purchaser's death, his widow would not be entitled to one-third of the property for life (her common-law dower rights). The dower trustee is never so called explicitly, but can be recognised either from the uses (see p.65), or from his description among the parties, for example 'William Townsend of Coventry, glazier, and Edward Lea of the same city, tailor, a person nominated by and in trust for the said William Townsend' [Coventry Record Office, TC/1/L/325]. He may be a separate party after the purchaser, or may be combined with the purchaser. It is also worth noting that dower trustees, unlike the trustees of settlements, do not usually enter into succeeding transactions, because the 'uses' include the ability for the real owner to dispose of the property. The dower trustee was no longer necessary after 1833, when dower could be 'barred' by a declaration in the deed itself. Later deeds often include the phrase 'who was a bachelor (or "unmarried") on 1 January 1834', to make clear the position in regard to dower. Another party frequently present in a release is the mortgagee— invariably so if the owner has mortgaged the property. In order to extinguish the mortgage satisfactorily, the purchaser may also have another trustee in whom the mortgage will be vested 'to attend the inheritance' (p.70).

Recital: One main concern is to justify the seller's title. Details of wills are often given, including the date of writing and of probate (and where it was proved). These should be recorded, because it is often informative to examine the complete will. It is noticeable how often deed bundles start with a will; it gave a particularly unassailable title, and no doubt lawyers were glad to lose sight of whatever had gone before. As already mentioned, the appointment of trustees is also recorded. This recital is particularly long and tedious for bankruptcy trustees, though, if the original bankruptcy deed is found, it may give interesting lists of the debts involved.

The second main concern of the recital is the mortgage (if any), usually including its establishment and some or all of its assignments. These repeat the mortgage deeds, and so can be ignored if they exist.

Finally, the agreement to purchase is often recited, perhaps with the date and place that the property was auctioned (to demonstrate that the sale was at full market rate). Sometimes the buyer at the auction had resold it to the final purchaser and this is explained; the first buyer may then be a party to the deed. The division of the purchase money between the co-owners, mortgagees and other recipients is also described.

Consideration: This clause tends to be short, with any more interesting details in the recital. People with minor interests in the property—trustees, widows resigning dower rights, etc.—generally received a nominal sum of 5s. each, which is noted in this clause.

Action: 'Hath granted, bargained, sold, alienated, released and confirmed, and by these presents doth grant, bargain, ..'

Property: See p.65.

Period: A conveyance of freehold by release is always 'for ever'. If the conveyance includes the assignment of a paid-off mortgage, then this will be assigned for the residue of the original term (often 1,000 years). A perpetual leasehold (see p.81) is often conveyed by lease and release. It will have the same 1,000-year period (usually), but can be distinguished from a mortgage because it is assigned to the purchaser, rather than to a trustee to 'attend the inheritance'; it can also be recognised in the recital.

Rent and tenure: If any rent has to be paid, it is usually included in the covenants. The tenure clause depends on the legal state of the property, but can be ignored for practical purposes.

Uses: Normally to the use of the purchaser, his heirs and assigns, i.e. with freedom to sell, mortgage or transfer the property, etc.; later, the dower trustee holds to the same uses. If, say, the money of a marriage settlement was used for the purchase, then the uses will be the same as in the settlement.

Covenants and conditions: These are generally formal, mostly intended to give the purchaser as strong a title as possible, and normally do not need to be studied in detail. They can include an agreement to levy a *fine*—'*sur cognisance de droit com ceo*' (see p.73)—or to execute any extra deed requested by the purchaser (sometimes within time or distance limits, e.g. without travelling 'more than ten miles' (1700), or 'outside the counties of Warwickshire or Staffordshire' (1692)). A warranty to defend the title may mention relatives of the vendor who do not appear elsewhere, and so need to be noted. Sometimes there are exclusions, either of a rent that has to be paid, or of a lease that has been granted and is still current.

One of the few important covenants arises when the seller is not handing over the previous title deeds. He then covenants firstly to produce copies if requested, and secondly to take reasonable care of, and produce on demand, the earlier deeds, as listed in a schedule at the bottom of the deed. These will have been described in an abstract of title, but, if that has disappeared, the schedule may give the only clue to the earlier history of the property. Schedules are rather difficult to interpret, as they usually only list the dates and parties, leaving one to guess if they are describing conveyances, mortgages, settlements, or whatever. Alternatively, this type of covenant might be made the subject of a separate deed (p.82).

Property: Property clauses can cover anything from an entire ducal estate to a strip of land six inches by 12 feet for the footings of a wall. Like the other clauses, part represents real information, while part is formal. Four property clauses will be quoted in detail, to illustrate their character and this distinction.

The first is a fairly simple example for rural property:

> All that quarterne or fourth parte of one yardland of arable, meadow, and pasture ground with the appurtenances, lying and being in the fields, precincts and territories of Napton upon the Hill in the said county of Warwickshire, and now or late in the tenure or occupation of the said Robert Crofts, his assignee or assignes, and heretofore purchased by the said Robert Crofts, deceased, uncle of the said Robert Crofts, party to these presents of and from one Elizabeth Greenoway and John Greenoway, Together with all and singular lands, leyes, hades, balkes, meadowes; pastures, lott grasse, parting grasse, feedings, comons and comon of pasture, profitts, commodityes, advantages, emoluments, and hereditaments whatsoever to the said quarterne ... belonging [1681; WRO, D19/591].

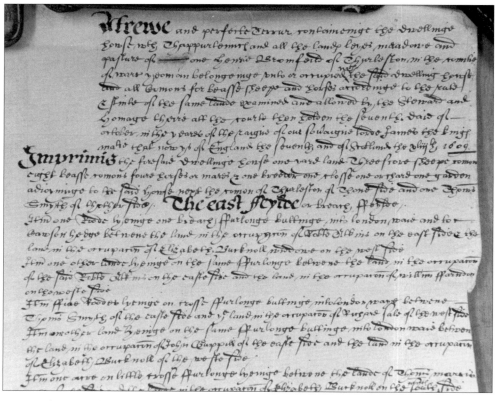

18   The start of a terrier of open-field lands in Thurlaston, Warwickshire, atttached to a deed of 1616. For text see p.105. [WRO CR2105/Box2/50]

Only the first part of this contains much useful information, though the second part suggests that common grazing rights were involved. It did not include a house, which would have been stated explicitly, as in the next example. The description of the number of yardlands or their fractions is typical of open-field land in dispersed strips. *Terriers* (detailed lists of strips) are occasionally included with deeds, especially if an open-field holding is being subdivided, and give very valuable topographical information (Illus.18).

The next example shows how enclosed fields might be described. The term 'messuage or tenement' is standard for a house, though occasionally 'tenement or cottage' is found for a small dwelling. As in the last example, the end of the property clause can be ignored.

One messuage and tenement with the appurtenances situate, lyinge and being within the parishe of Stoke Gabriell in the countie aforesaide [Devon], sometymes being but a bakehouse, barne, courtlage, garden, and orchard, and also certen parcells of land, meadow, and pasture with the appurtenances called the South Downes, the Millake, the Waleteane, and Waleteane meadow, conteyninge in the whole by estimacion five and twentie acres or thereabouts, be the same more or less, together with common in Myllake Green, all which premises are scytuate, lyinge and beinge in Stoke Gabriell aforesaid, now or heretofore parte and parcell or reputed to be parte and parcell of the Lordshippe or mannor of Paignton in the said countie of Devon, and now in the tenure, manurance [= *tenure*], or occupation of Gilbert Tully the elder, Gilbert Tully, son of Odes Tully, and Gilbert Kinge or one of them, their or one of their assignee or assignees, for and during their natural lives according to the custome of the said mannor of Paignton, And all houses, edifices, buildings, barnes, stables, shippens, courts, courtlages [courtyards], gardens, orchards, lands, meadows, lesowes, pastures, feedings, wasts, commons, common of pasture,wayes, pathes, waters, watercourses, easements, profits, commodities, annuities, and hereditaments whatsoever … [*etc. for several more lines*] [1637; WRO, L3/4].

Next comes a simple example for urban property, just recording the street in which the house lies and the occupier.

All that messuage, cottage, or tenement, garden, backside, hereditaments, and premises, situate, standing and being near a certain place called Saint James's Hill in the parish of Saint Mary in the Borough of Warwick, in the County of Warwick, formerly in the occupation of John Hill, and now of Edward Baron, And also … [*another house*], Together with all … [1784; WRO, CR1886/BB213].

The main description here occupies just one-and-a-quarter lines of text in the original, but the 'Together with' clause, covering every conceivable appurtenance possibly associated with the property, extends to no less than seven and a half long lines.

The final example shows how complex an urban property description could become, even without details about the building. It was probably made so precise to define clearly what part of the original larger plot was involved. The names of people owning adjoining houses (the abuttals) are often included in urban descriptions and are particularly helpful in locating property on the ground. The example also illustrates the concentration of a particular occupation in one part of a city. (For the full text of this deed, see p.110.)

All that messuage or tenement with the appurtenances called or knowne by the name of the Tolbooth, and heretofore in the several tenures or occupations of Thomas Hope, father of the said Samuel Hope, party to these presents, and John Holloway, clothworker, and heretofore part of a messuage or tenement sometime in the tenure of Elizabeth Sharratt, widdowe, which said messuage or tenement hereby granted is situate, lyinge and beinge in the City of Coventry aforesaid, in or neere a certaine streete there called or knowne by the name of Muche Parke Streete, between a messuage and yard there of one Samuel Clarke of Coundon in the said county of Warwickshire, gentleman, now or late in the tenure of Anthony Edwards, clothworker, on the north and west parts, and a messuage and garden there being the land of one Mary Coles, now in the occupation of Thomas Webb, clothworker, on the south part, and Much Parke Street aforesaid, on the East part, and conteyninge in breadth by the said streete side twenty three foote, and in breadth on the west side towards Anthony Edwards said yarte [sic] nineteene foote, and in length on the north side towards the said Anthony Edwards house thirty seaven foote, and in length on the south side towards the said messuage in the occupation of the said Thomas Webb fourty two foote With all houses, … [1678; in private ownership].

Other information that may be included in the property clause has been discussed in Chapter Two. In the 19th century, especially in the case of urban property, plans of the site and buildings may be found, with the phrase 'which said premises are more particularly delineated in the map or plan drawn in the margin of these presents'. In general, property descriptions were often unchanged from one deed to another, apart perhaps from amending the list of occupiers from, say, 'in the occupation of John Anstye', to 'formerly in the occupation of John Anstye, and now of Richard Porter'. It is not safe to deduce from such phrases that the former occupant had been there shortly before. Similarly, a phrase like 'newly rebuilt' can be repeated for a century!

MORTGAGE

Fundamentally, the mortgage is a lease for a long period at nominal rent, but it has three particular features: firstly, it is granted in consideration of a specified sum of money. Secondly, the deed will be cancelled if the money is repaid with interest by a certain date, but, if not, the mortgage becomes 'absolute'. At that moment, in theory the *mortgagee* (who lends the money) becomes owner of the property; in practice this very rarely happened. Thirdly, the property is still used by the mortgagor (the original owner); this is not stated in the deed. However, the last two points only became established during the 17th century, and before that mortgages had a very different character (p.11).

Various forms of deed are used for mortgages; the lease is the simplest, and has the following characteristics:

Parties: (1) The owner, i.e. the mortgagor, (2) the lender of the money, i.e. the mortgagee(s), who may be an individual or a group of trustees, executors of a will, etc. holding money in trust to invest.

Recital: Occasionally describes the owner's purchase. Usually states that he needs money, and that the mortgagee will lend it.

Consideration: The money being let (principal).

Action: 'Grant, bargain and sell and demise, set and to farm let' i.e. a mixture of a grant and a lease, of which the lease is the effective part.

Period: Usually 500 or 1,000 years 'without impeachment of waste' i.e. without the mortgagee being liable for any reduction in the value of the property. Terms of 99 years are found in the 17th century.

Rent: A peppercorn.

Conditions: The key clause in a mortgage, 'provided upon this express condition that if the said A (mortgagor) shall pay … [the principal and interest, at stated times], this present indenture of mortgage shall be *absolutely void*'. It continues, 'and if default shall be made [in repayment], it may be lawful for B (*mortgagee*) to enter on, have, hold, possess, and enjoy the same'. The form of repayment is also laid down. A sum of, say, £50 is typically either to be paid as £51 5s in six months, or as £1 5s in six months and £51 5s after a year. Both correspond to repayment with five per cent interest; the rate at any time in the 18th and 19th centuries hardly varied outside the range of four to five per cent, though it had risen to eight per cent in the mid–17th century.

In reality, both as a loan for the mortgagor and as an investment for the mortgagee, the mortgage was intended to continue indefinitely, with interest paid regularly. Indeed, during the course of the 17th century, the courts gradually established that mortgages could not be *foreclosed* (terminated) at the whim of the mortgagee, even if the date set for repayment had passed.[8] Thus they became a secure way for a property owner to obtain a loan without the danger of losing his land; he retained his *equity of redemption*, his right to repay the mortgage. The only way the mortgagee could foreclose was to apply to the Court of Chancery. A court order for the sale of the property would only be granted if the money due was not paid on the day set by the court.

In the 19th century, second mortgages appear, taken out on property already subject to one mortgage. These avoid the problem of default by including a 'power of sale' among the conditions, which meant that if the interest had been unpaid for a given time, say, six months, the mortgagee could (and often did) put the property up for auction, without needing a court order.

OTHER MORTGAGE DEEDS; ASSIGNMENT OF MORTGAGE

The previous example of a mortgage has the simple form of a lease for 1,000 years as a single indenture. Mortgages were also granted by lease and release, and even by fine. The release or the 'deed to lead the uses of the fine' (p.75) then contains the conditions for redemption and repayment.

As we have seen, even if the mortgagee wanted his money back, he could not foreclose. Instead, someone else was found to take over the mortgage, and a deed of *assignment of mortgage* was executed. To judge by the number of assignments that exist, there was no great difficulty in finding mortgage money, but the deeds themselves do not explain how this was done. The assignment is very like the assignment of a lease (p.61), with the following key clauses:

Parties: (1) The owner, (2) the original mortgagee (or perhaps his executors), (3) the new mortgagee; the parties may not, however, be in this order.

Recital: Date and details of the original mortgage and any earlier assignments. The original mortgage had usually become absolute (i.e. had passed its set redemption time), and this is often stated, as is the wish of the mortgagee to be repaid.

Consideration: The original principal, repaid to the old mortgagee. Sometimes the size of the mortgage was also increased.

---

[8] It was decided that, if the principal and interest were paid even belatedly, the mortgagee had obtained what he expected, the return of his money with interest, so that he had no right to take over the property.

Action: 'At the request and by the direction of A (the owner), B (the old mortgagee) hath bargained and sold, assigned and set over to C (the new mortgagee) … all the estate, right, title : … and number of years yet to come in . . .'

Property: Usually as in the original mortgage, but occasionally with the occupiers, etc. brought up to date; if new houses have been built, this may be noted to justify an increase in the value of the mortgage. Sometimes the property description is only given in full in the recital and this clause only notes 'the said messuage …'.

Conditions: The assigned mortgage is subject to the same conditions as the original one, and they are usually repeated.

THE END OF A MORTGAGE: ASSIGNMENT TO ATTEND THE INHERITANCE

The simplest way of terminating a mortgage was for the money to be repaid and a receipt endorsed on the back of the original deed. However, this was felt to be unsatisfactory. The 1,000 year lease had been granted and not properly terminated. Thus, what was adopted was an *assignment* of the mortgage (as just described) to a trustee for the owner *in trust to attend the inheritance*, with the following key phrase in the uses: 'to have and to hold to B (the trustee) … in trust for A (the owner), to wait upon and attend the inheritance'. This assignment may be incorporated in a release if the mortgage is being paid off at the same time as the property is sold, or may be a separate deed. In either case, the only new historical information is the name of the trustee, likely to be a friend of the owner. The deed also recites the original mortgage and the details of the property, which are valuable if the earlier deeds have not survived. In the later 19th century, with changes in the law, mortgages were paid off more simply; by reconveyance of the rights originally granted, and this was usually written on the back of the original deed.

If the mortgage could not be paid off, then the mortgagee might with difficulty enforce a sale (as noted above), or more usually the property would be put up for sale with the agreement of the owner. Occasionally, the mortgagee himself might buy it, in which case the owner would convey it to him by lease and release, releasing what was known as the *equity of redemption* (the right to repay the mortgage).

BOND

The bond does not have the form of an indenture, and it had many uses other than in relation to title deeds. However, it is often associated with a mortgage and so is conveniently described here. The bond has a characteristic appearance (Illus.19). The formal first section was in Latin until 1733, and was often printed. It simply states that one party is *bound* ('firmly bound and obliged') to pay a certain sum to the other party. The second part states that 'The condition of this obligation' is that, if a specified action is performed, then the first part will be void. This could be simply the payment of a stated sum of money at a stated time, as in the case of a straightforward debt, but bonds were also regularly used to strengthen a mortgage,

19 A 17th-century bond relating to the bequest of property in Greyfriars Lane, Coventry. For text see p.106. [WRO CR607/Coventry]

when the bond had the advantage that it could if necessary be enforced in a court of law, as an alternative to applying to foreclose the mortgage. By convention, the bond was for a *penal* sum, twice the amount actually due.

Bonds were also made to accompany conveyances. With these, the penal sum would be twice the purchase cost, and the seller would be bound either to give the purchaser 'quiet enjoyment' of the property, or to observe the 'covenants in a certain pair of indentures of even date' (i.e., a release executed on the same day as the bond). In the 17th century bonds often included a description of the property, but by the 18th century their only useful information is likely to be the names of the parties.

SETTLEMENTS

Two types of settlement are common among title deeds: the *family settlement* in which family property was entailed, i.e., assigned to trustees so that it would descend in the family ownership; and the *marriage settlement* in which property was held for the joint benefit of husband and wife and their children. Both take the form of conveyances to trustees, usually by lease and release in the 18th century, and by bargain and sale before then (see p.79).

The *marriage settlement* is generally the simpler type, with the following sections:
Parties: These include the husband and wife and a pair of trustees (one associated with the husband's family and one with the wife's). If either husband or wife is not the property-owner in his/her own right, then their parents or trustees also appear (e.g. the father whose son is being married). Sometimes, the settlement deed involves the purchase of a property, when its owner will be amongst the parties (confusingly, as he generally has nothing to do with the other persons concerned).
Recital: Usually commences 'Whereas a marriage has been arranged …' (a post-nuptial settlement, when the marriage had already taken place, was less common). The payment of money either as a marriage portion for the bride or by the husband's family is sometimes noted, but its omission does not necessarily mean that no dowry was involved.
Property: It can be important to remember that the property in the settlement often did not include everything owned by the husband. However, because the law held that anything owned by a wife was under her husband's control, all her property was likely to be listed in the settlement. In general, a balance was sought so that husband and wife contributed about equally to the settlement either in property or in money.
Uses: The uses to which the trustees are bound in a marriage settlement are normally fairly standard, and have four stages:
1. before the marriage, for whichever family originally owned the property;
2. jointly for husband and wife, and for the survivor after the death of his or her partner;
3. after the deaths of both parents, for the children of the marriage (sometimes in separate portions for elder and younger sons and daughters);
4. in the absence of children, to the heirs of the original owner (sometimes named).

Occasionally, a much simpler form is found in which the husband or wife after the other's death can assign the property as each chooses. This was probably used particularly for the marriage of an elderly woman when children were not expected.

Family settlements were often made for families of wealth and status, generation after generation, on such an occasion as the eldest son reaching the age of 21, or marrying.[9] Whenever a new settlement was made, the previous settlement would be annulled by a recovery (p.75). Their aim was to preserve the family estate intact for future generations, and they therefore arranged that the head of the family had the use (and profits) from the estate *during his life only*, and so could not sell it without the consent of both his heir and his trustees. Such a settlement is usually instantly recognisable because of its size! (Illus.4). Its principal sections are:

Parties: These include the father and eldest son, together with old and new trustees.

Recital: Of a previous settlement.

Property: Generally, most but not all of the family estate was covered, leaving a part that could easily be mortgaged or even sold if necessary. It was also possible for the trustees to mortgage the settled estate which presumably provided good security, though foreclosing would have been even more difficult than for an ordinary mortgage.

Uses: Although the property description in a family settlement can be lengthy, its bulk generally comes from the uses. The first concern has already been noted, to make the head of the family 'tenant for life', with his eldest son to succeed him (the 'tenant in tail'). The sequence after that had to be laid down, with 'remainders' to the eldest son's children in order; to his brothers and their children successively; to his sisters and their children—to the limit of the lawyer's patience and his client's purse. The settlement also provided an income for the owner's wife and lump sums for younger children. The details of these arrangements are usually of minor historical interest, although they indicate the financial strain placed on an estate by the children's portions. However, in the process of laying them down the settlement gives a clear view of the family, including for example the children's order of precedence.

FINES AND RECOVERIES

Of all the variety of deeds that are encountered, the fine and the recovery are the most extraordinary—and also the least useful. They are the official records of entirely formal legal cases, undertaken to confirm a change of ownership, or to cancel a previous deed. The clerks who wrote them had their own archaic styles of handwriting unlike those encountered in any other documents, and

---

[9] See B. English and J. Saville, *Strict Settlement: a Guide for Historians* (University of Hull, 1983).

20 Left- and right-hand Indentures of a Fine [Final Concord] of 1623 for Coventry. The black line shows how these joined to the Foot of Fine which was kept by the Court of Common Pleas and is now in the Public Record Office. For text see p.107. [WRO CR607/Coventry]

extremely hard to read. Worse, probably because the official record was open to anyone to inspect, the property description are formal and impossible to identify (e.g. 'two messuages, two gardens, one orchard, ten acres of land and two acres of meadow in Kenilworth'). Because of their formality, post-medieval fines and recoveries were always accompanied by private deeds giving full details of the transactions involved. Complete sets of fines and recoveries exist at the P.R.O., and are fully listed though they are exhausting to search except for short periods. Thus the individual documents themselves have little independent historical value though the complete sets can give information about land transactions in particular places.[10] Isolated fines where the associated deeds have not been preserved, are more useful as they record transactions which could otherwise only be found by an extensive search of the P.R.O. copies. Both fines and recoveries were abolished in 1833. Medieval fines are of considerably more historical significance and are discussed below (p.92).

1. *Fine; Deed to lead the uses of a fine*

The *fine* or *Final Concord* (so-called from its opening phrase: *Hec est finalis concordia* ..., meaning 'This is the final agreement') was the record of a case in the Court of Common Pleas. It was prepared in triplicate (see Illus.20), and the 'Feet of Fines'

---

[10] Readers should know that my dislike of these documents is not universally felt. A paper by F.G. Emmison in *The Local Historian* for September 1981 (no. 411) suggests that the acreages given are useful and fairly accurate and that the names of the parties can also be helpful. W.G. Hoskins, *The Midland Peasant* (1961), p.99f. uses a series of fines from 1586-7 to document the selling off of a substantial Leicestershire property to 16 freeholders.

were kept by the court (P.R.O. CP25).[11] Left and right 'indentures of fine' were for the plaintiff and defendant (called *querent* and *deforciant*), i.e. the purchaser and the seller. Because the seller had no use for his part, the purchaser often kept both copies. Occasionally deeds contain an *exemplification of a fine*, i.e. a copy prepared by the court of its record (the Foot of Fine); this looks like a recovery (see below), except that the text in the document is that of a fine.

After its opening phrase, the fine gives the date by regnal year and law term (Michaelmas (autumn), Hilary (spring), Trinity (summer)), then the names of the justices (which can be ignored). The main part runs '*Inter A, querent et B, deforciator de …* [the land]', or after 1733 'Between A, plaintiff and B, deforciant of …'. At the end, a fictitious sum is recorded, and B warrants to defend A's title. With a joint defendant, e.g. husband and wife, this warranty may indicate which of them was the original owner of the property.

The fine often accompanies either a conveyance or a mortgage: in either case, the main deed for the transaction would then include the agreement to levy a fine. Otherwise, a special deed was drawn up, called a *deed to lead the uses of a fine* (or, if the fine has already been levied, to *declare* its uses). This takes the form of an agreement with the following sections:

Parties: The seller and purchaser (for a sale). The plaintiff in the fine may well be a nominee or a trustee, and will then be included as a party.

Action: The deed 'witnesseth that in pursuance of covenants … it is covenanted, granted, and agreed' that A (the seller) will 'before the end of the next law term acknowledge and levy one Fine *sur cognizance de droit com ceo etc.* of (the property) … by the name or names of one messuage [as in the fine]'.

Uses: 'And it is agreed and declared that the cognizee (the plaintiff) shall be seized' to the uses listed.

A form of 'Deed to lead the Uses of a Fine' that is particularly intriguing is found in the later 17th century. It covers a whole collection of properties with their individual sellers and purchasers. Each transaction would have its own conveyance but all the parties joined together to levy a single fine, no doubt to reduce the expense, and they drew up a single *portmanteau deed* (my name) to lead its uses. This lists all the properties and their new owners, and the appropriate number of copies were prepared. Each therefore includes information about the whole set of unconnected people and property, for some of which other evidence may not have survived. With such a deed, it is therefore useful to record the different parties and property descriptions in detail.

2. *Recovery; Deed to make a tenant to the Precipe*

Fines were levied as a form of title insurance in relatively straightforward transactions, when the seller had a full legal right to dispose of the property. If it was entailed, i.e.

---

[11] To locate a Foot of Fine when the date and place is known is fairly easy, from the original lists arranged by Law Term and County (PRO IND1/17217-68); it is also not too tedious to collect fines for, say, Leicestershire for a reasonably short period, but to find possible fines for particular places over a wide range of dates is very onerous. Although some indexes do exist (IND1/17106-78), they are believed to be far from comprehensive. Feet of fines for the Palatinates of Chester, Durham and Lancaster are in CHES31, DURH12 and PL17 respectively.

21   Part of a Recovery of 1710 for property in Avon Dassett, Warwickshire [start of line 5],
showing an unusually clear example of the characteristic script. [WRO CR457/box5/bundle 6]

required by earlier deeds to descend in the family (see above, under 'Settlements')
before any sale or new family settlement could be effective, it was necessary to destroy
or *bar* the entail. This was achieved by a *Common Recovery* (Illus.21). The court action
in which the final owner 'recovered' the property was entirely formal, and the rolls
of the court's records (see p.41) merely state the stages by which his title was
established. The impressive document finally produced is the *exemplification*. This has
the form of a royal declaration in which the king states that the rolls of the Court
of Common Pleas for a particular year contain the recovery. The Latin version of the
preamble is given here, to help in finding the only useful part.

> **Warr'** [i.e., Warwickshire, but could be any county] A [the plaintiff in the case, called the
> demandant] **in propria persona petit versus** [in his own person demands against] **B** [the
> defendant, called the tenant] **decem messuagia** … [the property].

The description of the property is formal, but truthful as far as it goes, while A, the
demandant, may be the final recipient of the property; B is often the family lawyer. The
exemplification continues with a description of the court case. The recovery is sealed
with the seal of the Court of Common Pleas, usually enclosed in a tin box (a 'skippet').

As with a fine, a private deed was drawn up to explain the purpose of the
recovery. This could simply declare the uses of the recovery, but more often

involved a conveyance by lease and release. It was known as a 'Conveyance to make a tenant to the Precipe for the purpose of suffering a Common Recovery'. The property (fully described) was conveyed by the owner himself (who probably held it for life only) and his heir to B, a trustworthy third party, the 'tenant' (the *precipe* being the writ by which he would be summoned to court). Another party is the person who will carry out the recovery (the 'recoverer'), who is the family lawyer, or the purchaser or his lawyer if a sale is involved rather than the freeing of the property from an entail. The deed also includes:

Recital: the right of the owner and his heir to the property, and any agreement to purchase.

Consideration: The purchase money (if any), and nominal sums to the other parties, with the phrase 'for the docking, barring, defeating, and destroying all estates tail'.

Uses: The 'tenant' will hold the property 'as a good and perfect tenant', and a recovery will be carried out. The 'recoverer' will hold the property to whatever use is finally intended. As the uses come at the very end of the deed, they can be fairly easily located.

After 1833, if an entail was to be barred, it could be done by means of a straight-forward disentailing deed, though this had to be enrolled in the Court of Chancery.

The complete text of a recovery is not included here because of my strong view that wading through it will give no information worth the effort. However for those who wish to marvel at the contortions the legal mind could dream up, the sequence of events in a recovery is described below (adapted from a real example cited by Dibben). (See also Illus.27.)

1. A messuage and land held by John Shed as 'tenant for life' and his son Thomas as 'tenant in tail' is to be disentailed and sold to Robert Denny. They jointly convey the property to a lawyer Robert Baxter who becomes the 'tenant to the precipe'; this conveyance is not actually valid because the property is entailed. The same deed has another party, Stafford Squire, the recoverer, who will eventually hold it to the use of Robert Denny.

2. Stafford Squire starts a case against Robert Baxter in the Court of Common Pleas (asking for a writ of *precipe* to be served), claiming that the property was his, but that he, Stafford, had been illegally ejected (disseized) by one Hugh Hunt (a fictitious person), after which Robert Baxter had obtained possession.

3. In defending his title, Baxter calls on Thomas Shed to confirm his ownership (to *vouch to warranty*). Thomas, however, calls on a third party to vouch for the title, Francis Martin (who is the court crier); he is known as the *common vouchee*.

4. Stafford Squire and Francis Martin beg leave to 'imparle' (confer privately) before the case is heard. Stafford returns, but Francis does not come back into court when solemnly summoned.

5. Thus, Thomas Shed's and Francis Martin's support of Robert Baxter's title fail and judgement is awarded to Stafford Squire.

6. He therefore owns the property, held to the use of Robert Denny—the intended outcome. The exemplification of the court record is prepared and all retire to pay the lawyers' fees.

22   Part of Letters Patent of 1604 granting Warwick Castle to Fulke Greville. [WRO CR1886/BB404]

LETTERS PATENT (see Illus.22)

Royal grants were made by *letters patent* sealed with the Great Seal. They look like recoveries but have more legible writing, with a handsome royal portrait starting the first line. The majority of letters patent found with title deeds are of the 16th century, because this was the great period for the disposal of property obtained by the Crown at the dissolution of the monasteries. Small pieces of land were granted 'to be held in free socage, as of the manor of East Greenwich', and these could be bought and sold freely. However, complete manors were usually held of the Crown *in chief* (i.e. by feudal tenure), paying a modest annual rent. Permission was needed before they could be sold, and this was also granted by letters patent, giving a 'Licence to Alienate' the land.

Apart from the somewhat different appearance, the distinction between a letter patent and a recovery is also clear from its start, e.g.:

> Charles the Second … to all to whom these present letters shall come, greeting, Know ye that we for divers good causes … have given, and granted, and by these presents for us, our heirs and successors do give and grant unto our beloved Laurence Hide, esquire …

All letters patent are enrolled on the Patent Rolls (P.R.O. C66), and a long series of calendars has been published, extending to 1578 at present; these are always worth checking for any place of interest. The property descriptions are often detailed, including the names of occupiers (though rarely abuttals for urban property), and where monastic or guild property is concerned, the original owner is almost always stated. Some of the details may be omitted in the published calendars (though this is always noted), which may make it necessary to check the enrolled copies. It can also be useful to know that the details were usually based on the *Particulars for Grant* (P.R.O.E318), valuations for prospective purchasers. These in turn were taken from surveys of monastic property (see the P.R.O. 'List of Rentals and Surveys', *Lists and Indexes* vol. 25). It is not uncommon for errors to occur when the property description was copied from one document to another. Of these descriptions, those in the surveys are often the most useful because they show all the property of the original owner, which may not all have been granted to the same purchaser; they can also have valuable marginal notes indicating the purchasers of different parts of the property.

BARGAIN-AND-SALE; FEOFFMENT

These are forms of conveyance used especially in the 16th and 17th centuries before the lease and release became standard. They represent the development of medieval deeds following the Statute of Uses (1535); this is of great legal importance, but of less significance for the interpretation of straightforward deeds. The distinction between the bargain-and-sale and the feoffment lies not in their wording, but in the method used to render them valid.

1. *Feoffment*: The feoffment continues the medieval tradition in which the actual transfer of property only took place through the ceremony of livery of seizin, in which a token part of the property e.g. a key or a piece of turf, was handed over to the new owner in the presence of witnesses. The written deed merely confirmed the seizin.

   The post-medieval feoffment was written and signed first, but was only made effective by the seizin. Its form is straightforward, with *parties*; the *consideration* (often not stated in money terms); the *property*; and the *covenants* (usually concerned with providing a good title). The *action* clause is distinctive and reads 'given, granted, alienated, bargained and sold, and enfeoffed'. The seizin is recorded in an endorsement. The names of the witnesses are important historically, as they are the worthy neighbours who were present at the ceremony of seizin. This clause sometimes includes the witnessing of the deed, but a typical wording is as follows:

   > Memorandum that on the tenth day of August in the yeare of our Lord God first within written, quiet and peaceable possession, together with livery and seisin of all and singular the said premises was given and delivered to the within-named John Kemsey in his proper person to hold to him and his heirs and assignes forever, according to the tenor and effect of these presents, in the presence of Thomas Wyse, The marke of John Hill the younger, Alexander Dougan, John Courte [1657; WRO, CR1886/5687, slightly edited].

2. The *enrolled bargain-and-sale* was created by the Statute of Enrolments (1535), as an alternative to the feoffment; the bargain-and-sale itself had existed previously but transferred only the use of the property, not its ownership. The text differs from the feoffment only in its action clause, 'granted, alienated, bargained and sold'. The main distinction is that it was valid without seizin, but had to be enrolled within six months either by the royal courts at Westminster (usually on the Close Rolls), or by the Clerk of the Peace for the county, on rolls forming part of the Quarter Sessions records (see p.40). The enrolment of the deed is always recorded in an endorsement giving the date when this was done, e.g. '*Irrotulatur in dorso clausarum Cancellarie ...*' ('enrolled on the dorse of the Close roll of Chancery').

Landowners disliked both the bargain-and-sale and the feoffment because of their publicity. Either the seizin ceremony, or the enrolled and publicly available copy left no secrecy about their actions. This was the reason that the lease and release became the principal form of conveyance, because it provided a deed that was secure and at the same time secret. Occasionally, deeds of bargain-and-sale are seen without either seizin or an endorsement of their enrolment. Some of these concern such small pieces of property (e.g. half a well), that presumably nothing more formal was thought necessary. Others seem at first to be legally invalid but on a careful look they turn out to be counterparts. Rather than the conveyance by A to B, signed by A, they are duplicates signed by B, and kept by A to confirm that B would observe any covenants involved; such counterparts were also retained as a record that A had sold the property. In other cases, the non-enrolled bargain-and-sale was accompanied by a feoffment or *quitclaim* with seizin.

QUITCLAIM

Quitclaims are occasionally found among 16th- and 17th-century deeds, and like feoffments are medieval in origin. They are not difficult to understand in themselves, but it is not always obvious why they were used. Their actual function was to *release* or *quitclaim* the rights of the first party to the second party, and some concern the possible rights of someone who was not actually the property owner. Others are endorsed with livery of seizin and were used as feoffments. Quitclaims are not indented, and are rather more often in Latin than other post-medieval deeds, starting '*Omnibus Christi fidelibus ...*'. In English their opening phrase becomes:

> To all Christian people to whom this present writing shall come I, [A], send greeting in the Lord everlasting, Know ye that I for divers good cause have remised, released and for ever quitclaimed unto [B] all estate, right, title ... of me the said A, in ... [the property].

An alternative wording is 'Know all men by these presents ...', continuing broadly as before.

PERPETUAL LEASE

This 17th-century type of deed is relatively uncommon, but worth describing, particularly as examples are easily confused with mortgages (sometimes even in record office lists). Although technically leases, they have the effect of conveyances, because they last for a very long time, often 500 or 1,000 years (and thus can conveniently, though loosely, be called 'perpetual'). As with quitclaims, the reason for their use is unclear, but they probably represent another way to avoid the problems of the bargain-and-sale, because only the leasehold interest is being transferred. They also have some similarity to grants in fee farm (see p.90), which are sometimes found in the post-medieval period; these are conveyances *for ever*, but with a substantial 'fee farm' rent reserved, to be paid to the seller. The distinctive features of a perpetual lease are:

Action: 'Demise, set and to farm let', as for other leases.

Period: Usually 500 or 1,000 years.

Rent: Some small sum, e.g. 5s, but not simply a peppercorn.

Covenants: In contrast to a mortgage, the perpetual lease does not have a provision for redemption.

COPIES OF COURT ROLL

All the deeds so far described were used for freehold land, perhaps covering three-quarters of all property in England by the 17th century. However, in a considerable number of places, land was held by *copyhold*, for which the title deed was the *copy* of an entry on the manor court roll. Many such copies survive in bundles of title deeds but the primary record of the copyholder's title was in the manor court rolls. For this reason, although the appearance of copies of court roll has been described above so that they can be recognised, they are discussed in detail in a separate section below (p.94); a medieval and a post-medieval copy of court roll are shown in Illustrations 25 and 28.

MISCELLANEOUS POST-MEDIEVAL DEEDS

A variety of other deeds may occasionally be encountered, and a few should be mentioned. **Deeds of Partition** and **Deeds of Exchange** are rather similar. Each uses the lease and release form, with two copies of an identical release (one for each party) describing two separate transfers of property, one from A to B, the other from B to A. Each party also executes a lease for a year to the other, but these are different, each concerning one of the two pieces of property which are either being partitioned or exchanged.

A **Deed of Enfranchisement** was used to convert a copyhold into a freehold. It has the normal indenture form. The lord of the manor, in return for a substantial consideration 'for the freeing and extinguishing of the copyhold tenure from all copyhold services, fines and heriots', granted the specified property, to he held 'for ever', subject only to the payment of the rent and to attendance at the manor court.

A **Covenant to Produce Deeds** was executed when a seller retained some or all of the title deeds, usually because they also related to other property. The covenant has an action clause, 'doth covenant and agree', to produce the deeds, and in addition it recites the sale of the property, including a full description. At the end, a schedule of the deeds to be produced is given, similar to those occasionally included in a Release (see p.65).

Articles of Agreement usually have a heading identifying them, followed by a series of numbered clauses. They are fairly easy to follow as they describe what was actually intended before it was converted into the legal language of the deed itself. Agreements for a marriage settlement are perhaps the most common, followed by those for the purchase of a property.

Contracts are occasionally found in deed bundles, concerning building work in particular, and they can be extremely interesting. They have the form of indentures between A, the landowner, and B, a carpenter or mason in which B agrees to erect a building to a stated specification and timetable and A will pay him agreed sums of money at stated times. They also normally include agreements for arbitration in the event of dispute.

Two documents are not considered in detail here, because they are financial rather than directly concerned with property. The **Recognisance in the nature of a Statute Staple** was a strong form of bond, more readily enforced if necessary. It was usually cancelled by a separate document, a **Defeazance of a Recognisance**.

MEDIEVAL DEEDS
INTRODUCTION

Before medieval deeds can be understood, two barriers have to be overcome, the writing and the language. As compensation, their text and structure are much simpler than for most post-medieval deeds, so that extracting their historical evidence is generally less difficult. Record offices have also tended to calendar and index their medieval deeds in preference to later ones, often providing an outline to start from. For the handwriting, various guides exist (see Further Reading) of which the book by Newton is by far the best for medieval deeds (though unfortunately out of print); those by Grieve and Hector are also to be recommended, but cover a wider range, with less specifically medieval material. One particular problem is that abbreviations were used on every possible occasion. C.T. Martin, *The Record Interpreter* (reprinted Phillimore, 1982) is useful as an aid to deciphering them, and also as a Latin vocabulary, while E. Gooder, *Latin for Local History* (Longmans, 1978) and Denis Stuart, *Latin for Local and*

Family Historians (Phillimore, 1995) are helpful for Latin translation. They include deed texts which can be matched with examples being studied. Sometimes deeds are written in English, and these are always intriguing though not necessarily easier to understand. For the rare documents in Norman French, it is reasonable to ask for expert help, particularly as most are unusual in content as well as language.

DATING

The earliest surviving deeds are Anglo-Saxon charters, which are almost exclusively royal grants. Charters issued by the nobility appear in the 12th century, though their texts generally do not follow standard later forms. Most of them have been preserved because they granted substantial property or rights to important beneficiaries (especially monasteries), and their study is bedevilled because these recipients were not above 'improving' their charters, or even producing completely spurious deeds; their forgeries were not necessarily designed to obtain property that did not belong to them, but rather to recover what had been lost in troubled times, and to reinforce their ownership (perhaps when their charters had been destroyed). Detection of forgeries is not made easier because many are only preserved in cartularies or as enrolled deeds (pp.39-43). No recent publication has examined 12th-century charters as a whole, so there is little to help with the interpretation of individual examples. However, an informative discussion of the development of written charters and of the problem of forgeries is given by M.T. Clanchy, *From Memory to Written Record* (1993).

Deeds in standard medieval form appear at the beginning of the 13th century.[12] Some were issued by people of modest status, including burgesses in towns and freeholders in the country. We rarely know exactly when they were written. The inclusion of dates in deeds only became standard practice in about 1300, and much later undated deeds are occasionally found. The earliest deeds that regularly include dates are leases for specific periods of time (e.g. seven years), when it was obviously important to state when the lease started. A good example is in Illustration 1 (p.3); as here, such early deeds are usually not dated themselves, but can be assumed to have been written when the lease started.

With undated deeds, a very approximate date can be obtained from the handwriting (e.g. by matching it with examples in palaeography texts). The only way to achieve greater accuracy is from the people named as parties and witnesses in the deed. If prominent men are involved, the dates of their death may be known, giving limiting dates. Otherwise, to make progress a moderately large number of deeds needs to be studied. The earliest dated ones will include names also found in undated deeds, which therefore cannot be very much earlier. These deeds in turn will contain other names which cannot be directly dated, but must somewhat

---

[12] See C. A. F. Meekings and P. Shearman (eds.), 'Fitznells Cartulary', *Surrey Record Society*, vol. 26, cxl, for a survey of the changing patterns found in medieval deeds, illustrated from a Surrey archive.

Edges	Seal	Type of Deed	Plate
Straight	Suspended on tag	Gift or quitclaim	24
Indented top	Suspended on tag	Lease or counterpart; Agreement	1
Indented side and top		Fine	(as 20)
Straight	On sideways tongue	Bond;* Letter of Attorney	23

* A medieval bond has its condition on the dorse.

Table 10 Shapes of medieval deeds.

precede the last group. In this way, with the help of a few fixed points, a framework can be built up to provide dates with an accuracy of about a generation (see also p.30 for the application of computers to this problem).

When the text of a deed contains a date, this is hardly ever in modern style, and it needs to be interpreted. The year is normally given as the 'regnal year' (p.52), while until the mid-15th century, the day is hardly ever specified by the day of the month. Instead, it is related to a church festival, e.g. 'Wednesday before the Feast of Saint Martin, in the year of the reign of King Edward, the third after the conquest, the twenty fourth'. In working out such problems, C.R. Cheney's *Handbook of Dates* is indispensable. First, the table of regnal years gives 24 Edward III as 25 January 1350 to 24 January 1351, and refers to calendar tables 7 (for 1350) and 27 (for 1351). Then, the list of saints' days (which includes all the likely day and festival names as well) gives St Martin's Day as 11 November.[13] Calendar table 7 shows that, in 1350, 11 November was a Thursday, so the deed was dated 10 November 1350. The procedure is the same for dates relating to the moveable Church feasts (Easter, Whitsun, Trinity, etc.), except that their dates have to be found from the calendar tables themselves. Two special terms are *in vigilia* and *in crastina*, respectively the day before and day after the feast.

SHAPE AND PATTERN
Medieval deeds are much shorter than post-medieval ones, hardly ever larger than a smallish piece of parchment. In physical shape they have one of the forms listed in Table 10:

Medieval leases and other indented documents (agreements, etc.) were always produced by cutting up a single sheet of parchment (unlike post-medieval ones). Occasionally both parts survive and can be fitted together; the word *'cirographum'* is often written across the join, and these indented documents are therefore sometimes called 'chirographs'. A bond or a letter of attorney has its seal attached to a strip cut from the bottom of the sheet of parchment, and it should have another thin strip at the very bottom, though often this has been torn off. These deeds were formally private rather than public, and so were designed to be folded and tied up with this strip (see Illus.23).

---

[13] Care is needed because several saints of the same name may exist, while many major saints have several feast days. Here, the major St Martin (of Tours) can be assumed.

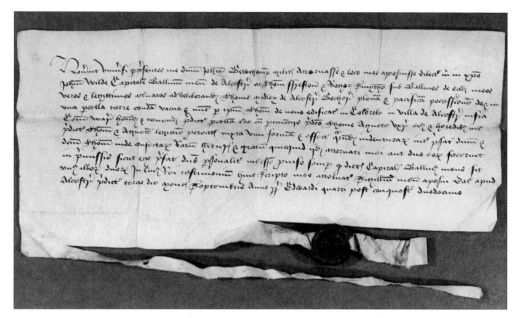

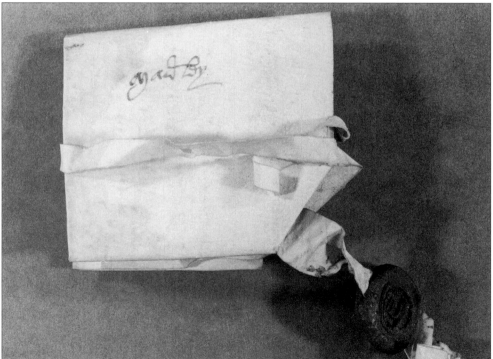

23 Medieval letter of attorney of 1472 relating to a transfer of property in Alcester, Warwickshire (a) open (b) closed, showing how the second strip of parchment (often torn off) was wrapped around the folded letter, leaving the seal showing for authentication. For text see p.108. [WRO CR1886/113]

Type of deed	Normal start	Action
Gift (conveyance)	*Sciant presentes et futuri* Know (all men) present and future	*Dedi, concessi et hac presenta carta confirmavi* have given, granted, and by this present charter confirmed
Quitclaim (three alternative starts)	*Omnibus Christi fidelibus* To all the faithful in Christ *Pateat Universis per Presentes* Be it known by these presents *Noverint Universi* Know all men	*Remisisse, relaxasse, et quietclamasse* Remise, relax and quitclaim The initial phrases often continue *ad quod hoc presens scriptum pervenit* (to whom this present writing comes)
Lease	*Hec indentura facta inter* This indenture made between (occasionally starts as quitclaim)	*Concessuit et dimisuit* have conceded and leased
Fine	*Hec est Finalis Concordia* This is the final agreement	Indicated by the first phrase
Letter of Attorney	Generally as second or third quitclaim forms	*Attornasse et in loco meo possuisse* ... *dilectos in Christo* Attorn and in my stead place ... beloved in Christ
Bond	As last	*firmiter teneri et obligari* Am firmly bound and obliged
Agreement	*Hec conventio facta inter* This agreement made (or sometimes as leases)	Indicated by this first phrase or by *conventio* in the text

Table 11 Initial words and 'action' clauses of medieval deeds.

As well as their shape, the first words of medieval deeds are useful in suggesting at a glance the sort of medieval deed being examined (see Table 11). The full identification comes from the *action* clause but this can be difficult to spot, as it is not picked out with capital letters.

CLAUSES

Like post-medieval deeds, the texts of medieval deeds are arranged systematically in clauses. The most common arrangement can best be illustrated by an actual example, a Deed of Gift (see Illus.24) with its translation, divided up to show the various clauses in the deed. After this the special features of the individual types of deed will be considered.

EXAMPLE OF A DEED OF GIFT
Introduction: *Sciant presentes et futuri* (Know all men present and to come)
First party: *quod ego Willelmus Tebowde de Westun Undyrwode* [Bucks] (That I William Tebowde of Weston Underwood)
Action: *Dedi, concessi et hac presenti carta mea confirmavi* (Have given, granted and by this my present charter confirmed)

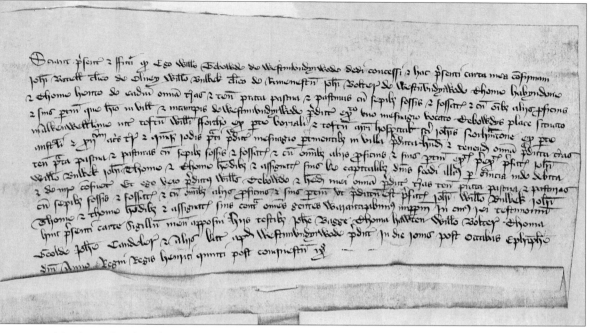

24 A medieval Gift [conveyance] of 1422, transferring land in Weston Underwood, Buckinghamshire. For text see p.86f. [WRO CR1998/J1/533C]

Second party: *Johanni Batell, clerico de Olney, Willelmo Bulbek, clerico de Ravenestun, Johanni Bolter de Westun Undyrwode, Thome Hobyndone et Thome Hento de eadem* (To John Batell, clerk of Olney, William Bulbek, clerk of Ravenstun, John Bolter of Weston Underwood, Thomas Habyndone and Thomas Hent of the same) [The presence of several grantees, including chaplains, makes it likely that they were trustees (feoffees) for the real owner; in medieval deeds, unlike later ones, the reason for a gift being made to a group of feoffees is hardly ever stated. The surname of the last party was probably Hent, with the form Hento representing the dative case.]

Property: *Omnia terras et tenementa, prata, pascua et pasturas cum sepibus, fossis et fossatis et cum omnibus aliis proficuis et suis pertinentiis quod habeo in villa et in campis de Westun Undyrwode predicto, excepto uno mesuagio vocato Tebowdys Place situato in Alkenwelllane inter toftum Willelmi Fortho ex parte boriali et toftum Magistri Hospitalis Sancti Johannis Norhamtone ex parte australi, et duodecim acris terre et quinque rodis prati, predicto mesuagio pertinentibus in villa predicta* (All lands and tenements, meadows, grazing land and pasture, with their hedges, banks and ditches, and with all profits and their appurtenances which I have in the village and fields of Weston Underwode aforesaid, except one house called Tebowdys Place, situated in Alkenwell Lane, between the toft [house plot] of William Forth [Fortho probably being the ablative form] on the north side, and the toft of the Master of the Hospital of Saint John [in] Northampton on the south side, and 12 acres [arable] land and five rods of meadow, belonging to the said messuage in the said village

Tenure: *Habendum et tenendum omnia predicta terras, tenementa, prata, pascua, et pasturas cum sepibus, fossis et fossatis et cum omnibus aliis proficuis et suis pertinentiis exceptis pre-exceptis prefatis Johanni, Willelmo Bulbek, Johanni, Thome et Thome heredibus et assignatis suis, de capitalibus dominis feodi illius* (To have and to hold all the said lands ..., except as before excepted, to the said John, William Bulbek, John, Thomas and Thomas, their heirs and assigns, from the chief lords of that fee)

Rent and service: *Per servicia inde debita et de iure consueta* (By the service thence due [from the property], and of right accustomed)

[**Term**: either before or after the rent, but absent in this example. When a limited period is not involved *in perpetuum* (forever) is normal.]

[**Conditions**: Conditions may be imposed, particularly concerning the future ownership of the property.]

Warranty: *Et ego vero predictus Willelmus Tebowde et heredes mei omnia predicta terras, tenementis, prata, pascua, et pasturas cum sepibus, fossis et fossatis et cum omnibus aliis proficuis et suis pertinentiis ut predictus est prefatis Johanni, Willelmo Bulbek, Johanni, Thome et Thome, heredibus et assignatis suis, contra omnes gentes Warantizabimus in perpetuum.* (And I truly the said William Tebowde and my heirs, all the said lands ..., as aforesaid, to the said John, William Bulbek, John, Thomas and Thomas their heirs and assigns, will warrant for ever.)

[**Consideration**: Occasionally included, especially in early deeds, usually near the end of the deed]

Attestation and witnesses: *In cuius rei testimonium huic presenti carte sigillum meum apposui, Hiis testibus Johanne Bagge, Thoma Hawten, Willelmo Bolter, Thoma Goolde, Johanne Candeler et aliis.* (In witness of which thing I have affixed my seal to this my present charter, These being witnesses, John Bagge, ... and others.)

Date: *Data apud Westun Undyrwode predicto in die Jovis post octavas Ephiphanie Domini, anno regni regis Henrici quinti post conquestum nono* (Dated at Weston Underwood, Thursday after the octave [period of eight days including and after the feast] of Epiphany [6 January], the ninth year of the reign of King Henry the fifth after the Conquest [15 January 1422] [WRO, CR1998/J1/553C].

Seal: [The deed carries the seal of William Tebowde, with a rose design, and an illegible inscription.]

Deeds were authenticated by the seal or seals of the first party. These were much studied in the 19th century, but have been neglected since then. Interest in them has recently revived, in such aspects as their artistic style, the social status of people owning seals, and the relationship between this and the character of the seal. It is notable that women usually had their own seals, so a grant by husband and wife together had two seals. Occasionally seals were borrowed, and people living far from the property being sold sometimes used their local town seal, declaring in the deed that their own seal would not be known to the purchaser. Thus, a study of the seal in context can throw considerable light on the parties involved in the transaction.].[14]

---

[14] See especially, P.D.A. Harvey and A. McGuinness, *A Guide to British Medieval Seals* (British Library and Public Record Office, 1996). An interesting survey of seals is D.H. Williams, *Welsh History through Seals* (National Museum of Wales, 1982). See also H. Jenkinson, *Guide to Seals in the Public Record Office* (H.M.S.O. 1968).

TYPES OF MEDIEVAL DEED

GIFTS

The main medieval deed is the *gift*, the permanent transfer of property from one person to another. Although the price paid is not often stated, the name does not imply a free gift, but is the technical term, contrasted to a *grant* of anything other than property, e.g. goods or the right to tithes. Gifts to monasteries or churches are often distinguished as being *in pura elimosina* (in pure alms), and these were made without any recompense to the giver.

The normal pattern of a gift is illustrated in the example just given. The key points for recognition are the initial phrase and the *action*, signalled by the words '*dedi, concessi* ...' This is always in the past tense (in contrast to post-medieval deeds), showing that the deed is a formal record of an action that has already been completed. The actual transfer of ownership took place by giving and taking *seizin* (cf. p.79). Unlike later feoffments, medieval gifts rarely record the ceremony on the back of the deed.

Parties: These are usually straightforward. If the grantor is a woman, she is described as making her grant '*in pura viduetate*' (in pure widowhood), or '*in pura virginitate*', as only widows or spinsters could dispose of their own property. Almost always the former husband or the father of the grantor is named as well. More complicated family connections are also often recorded (see p.19).

Property: The descriptions in medieval deeds tend to be less detailed than later. They often list the features of the property, house, croft, arable land, pasture, etc., without more detail, as in the example. Occasionally open field land is fully described, with each strip listed, furlong by furlong,[15] with the owners of the strips on each side; this is very valuable for the study of agrarian history, and for the information it gives on minor names. To counterbalance this, other deeds say no more than 'all my land in X'. Descriptions giving the number of acres or subdivisions (one acre = four rods = 40 perches) need particular care in their interpretation. Not only were acres of different sizes in different places (e.g. the Cornish acre was five-sixths of a statute acre), but individual open field strips were sometimes described as 'acres'.

The second part of the example uses *abuttals* to describe the house that was not to be conveyed—the names of the owners or occupiers of the adjoining properties. Abuttals are very common in medieval deeds for urban houses, but the inclusion of the name of the tenant of the property being transferred is rare (the reverse of post-medieval practice). The abuttals are not always consistent, which can cause difficulty in matching descriptions. For example, deeds for a Coventry house which could be firmly identified from other evidence had the abuttals listed in Table 12 on one side.[16]

Out-of-date names were often used, as here, probably to strengthen the identification with earlier documents. Tenants are also often named in abuttals.

---

[15] The subdivisions of a village's open field, each containing a group of aligned strips.

[16] From an unpublished study by the author. The deeds used are mainly in the P.R.O. Ancient Deeds A-series.

Date	Abuttal
*c.*1300	Land of Robert de London
*c.*1300	Land of Robert de Kenilworth (and in a deed of 1317 for the property itself Robert le Keu of Kenilworth and Alice his wife)
1314	Land of Robert le Keu and Alice his wife
1331	Tenement sometimes of Master Robert Cokus (given in the genitive as Coki) (These four are believed to be identical; le Keu means cook, i.e. Cokus)
1359	Tenement John Luke holds (as tenant)
1361	Tenement sometime of Master Robert Cokus
1365	Tenement John Luke holds
1377	Tenement that was of Richard Tole (owner in the 1340s)
1393	Tenement John de Wedon holds (life tenant from 1377)

Table 12 Abuttals of a Coventry house.

Tenure: The most important distinction depends on whether the deed dates from before or after 1290, when the statute '*Quia Emptores*' (meaning 'Because purchasers', the first words of the statute) was passed. Before this, in a grant from A to B the property was usually held 'of me [A] and my heirs' by some particular rent or service. Thus this grant introduced a new link in the chain of feudal tenure: B held of A, who was a 'mesne' or intermediate tenant who held of X, the 'chief' or superior lord who held from the king (perhaps via other mesne tenants). If A did not pay his rent to X, X would find it difficult to collect because A was no longer in possession of the property. After 1290, any grant had to be made to B, to hold 'of the chief lord', i.e. B would hold directly from X, who would then be able to collect the services due.

Rent and service: The standard late medieval phrase was 'by the service due and of right accustomed'. In 13th-century deeds, these chief rents are occasionally specified, sometimes including two or three separate rents to different people (each created by a former grant). Most of the payments were of money, rents of a few shillings which may at one time have represented the value of the property. Others were rents in kind, e.g. a pound of pepper or of cumin (both valuable spices), while some were formal acknowledgements, such as 'a red rose at Midsummer,' or 'a clove of gillyflower [the early name for cloves] at Easter'.

In theory, after 1290 no further chief rents were created, but occasional deeds dating from a little later still include them. At the end of the medieval period and later, grants were made that reserved a *fee-farm rent* (a perpetual rent charge); these grants include a condition allowing the grantor to *distrain* (seize goods) if the rent is unpaid. These rents were in effect the same as the old chief rents, but were not so called.

Conditions: The only common conditions in gifts are those reserving the succession of the property to the heirs of the grantee, usually also with *remainder* to the heirs of the grantor.

Warranty: The warranty clause, starting '*Et ego*' or '*Et nos*' is standard in medieval deeds. However, it is occasionally absent from very early deeds (early 13th-century and before), and this can be a help in dating.

Consideration: This is occasionally included in 13th-century deeds (rarely thereafter), with a phrase like '*Et pro hac donacione* (B) *dedit* (A) *decem marcas*' (And for this gift B gives A ten marks: one mark was worth 13s. 4d.).

Witnesses: The witnesses in medieval deeds deserve careful study. In a village, they will be the most respected inhabitants, while in a town they generally start with the mayor or a leading burgess. The lesser witnesses include people living near or next to the property involved, who could vouch directly for the transaction. The witness lists therefore help locate both the property and the inhabitants in the town. Early deeds often identify witnesses genealogically, e.g. 'A the brother (or the son) of B', while the dates at which witnesses appear and disappear are evidence for their life span. The final witness in early deeds, before the universal 'and many others' is often a priest, e.g. 'Roger *clericus*'. He was probably the actual scribe of the deed, though this needs to be confirmed by comparing the writing styles in deeds witnessed by the same man.[17]

QUITCLAIMS

These are perhaps even commoner than gifts, because medieval purchasers were very concerned to make their ownership proof against any attack. In particular there was a general feeling that property should only pass by inheritance, even if it was not formally held *in tail*. Thus a purchaser might be sued for wrongful occupation by a relative of the grantor. The new owner would therefore obtain a quitclaim which was a disclaimer of interest in the property from anyone who might be expected to make a claim in the future, such as the grantor's father or mother, brother or son. The grantor himself often executed a quitclaim as well as his gift.

The initial phrases of quitclaims (p.86) take various forms, but with little difference in meaning. The key section is the *action* indicated by the words '*Remisisse, relaxasse, et omnio pro me et heredibus meis quietclamasse*' (I[A] remise, relax, and quitclaim everything for me and my heirs) yielding to B '*totum ius et clameu quod habui vel habere potui*' (all right and claim I had or might have). The property is described in the same words as in the corresponding grant. The remainder of the quitclaim merely repeats the action clause in other words. The witnesses are sometimes preceded by a statement of the consideration given by B to A.

LEASES

Leases are the most frequent type of medieval indented deed, and correspondingly they usually start '*Hec indentura ...*', though other phrases are found. Indentures were also used for other deeds, particularly agreements (see p.93). The full standard opening clause is '*Hec indentura facta inter* [A] *ex parte una et* [B] *ex parte altera testatur quod ...*' (This indenture made between A of the one part and B of the other part witnesses that ...). The next phrase describes the action. A '*concessuit et dimisuit*' (has

[17] See J.H. Hodson, 'Medieval charters: the last witness', *J. Soc. Archivists*, vol.5(2) (1974), pp.71–89.

conceded and leased) the property to B. Leases continue with clauses for tenure, rent, and period. Medieval leases were made either for terms of years, or for the life of the recipient. Some life leases, however, were effectively for a period of years. They might allow the heirs of the tenant to continue the lease if he should die within, say, ten years. Others increased the rent to a penal value after a number of years; although the tenant could retain possession, it was not worthwhile. Leases for the life of the grantor imply that he himself had only a life interest.

The last section of a lease before the witnesses generally contains several *conditions*. Most are standard, providing for distraint or re-possession if the rent is not paid, and for the tenant to keep the property in good repair. The owners usually give a *warranty* to the tenants for the term of the lease. More interesting and unusual conditions are occasionally found, and are worth particular attention. They include building agreements, which can give important evidence about the types of buildings in use.[18] Sometimes part of the property is reserved for the grantor (e.g. a chamber and use of the fire in the hall for cooking), or special payments in kind are made for his maintenance. These throw light on both social conditions and household structure.

FINES

Medieval fines or final concords are exactly the same in form and function as later ones (described fully on p.73), with one crucial difference. Post-medieval fines were always produced as part of a transaction which is explained in more detail in an accompanying deed, whilst medieval fines mostly stand on their own as the only record of a property transfer. Thus they are more important as evidence and should not be ignored, even though the property is described in general terms (as in post-medieval examples); the financial considerations are apparently fictitious, except perhaps in the earliest examples. Feet of Fines exist in the P.R.O. from 1195, though fines were made before this, and a few earlier originals or copies survive. For a fair number of counties, some or all of the medieval fines have been published.[19]

Original medieval fines should be looked at closely, even apart from their greater significance as evidence. In many boroughs, the town court had or claimed the right to conduct the fictitious actions which produced fines. The resulting documents start '*Hec est finalis concordia facta in curia libertatis ville de …*' (This is the final concord made in the court of the liberty of the town of …). They generally continue with the statement that they were transferred there from the court at Westminster. This will have left traces in the records of the Court of Common Pleas, but buried among mountains of unindexed material, and the fines themselves are naturally not among the Feet of Fines. In principle the feet of these fines should be among the borough records, but they may well not have survived. Therefore, if an original fine was not levied at Westminster, it should be fully recorded.

---

[18] For examples, see L.F. Salzman, *Building in England down to 1540* (Oxford, 2nd ed. 1967).

[19] Jonathan Kissock, 'Medieval feet of fines: a study of their uses with a catalogue of published sources', *Local Historian* May 1994, pp.66-82 gives a list of published medieval fines and examines their use. See also E.L.C. Mullins, *Texts and Calendars*, vols.1 and 2, Royal Historical Society, 1958; 1983.

OTHER MEDIEVAL DEEDS

Various other types of deeds are occasionally found, and some should be mentioned. Perhaps the most common is the **Letter of Attorney** (Illus.23). The ceremony of seizin played a vital part in the transfer of property, but on occasion the vendor or the purchaser could not take part in person. He would therefore appoint a substitute, either to give or to receive seizin on his behalf. The appointment was made by a formal letter, which was kept with the title deeds. The following initial clause identifies them: '*Pateat universi per presentes me* [or an equivalent] [A] *attornasse et in loco meo posuisse dilectos in Christo* [B] ...' (Know all by these presents that I A do attorn and in my stead place the beloved in Christ B ...). The next clause depends on whether the person appointed was to give or receive seizin. The first typically reads '*meos veros et legitimos attornatos ad deliberand* [C] *plenam et pacificam possessionem de et in* [the property]' (for me truly and legitimately attorn to deliver to C full and peaceable possession of and in ...). An example of the alternative is '*ad recipiend in nomine meo plenam et pacificam sezinam in* ...' (to receive in my name full and peaceful seizin in ...). The final important section is the *property description*, which is usually in the same words as the main deed for the transaction. Thus, the letter of attorney can serve as a substitute for this.

Particularly in towns, **Agreements** were needed between neighbours. They generally start either as an indenture, or with the words '*Hec conventio facta inter* [A] *et* [B]' (This agreement made between A and B), and continue with the details of the agreement. They concern such matters as permission to install and repair a gutter, or to overhang the adjoining property. Some agreements mention a payment from one party to the other, or a yearly rent, but often they were of benefit to both sides, and no money was involved.

RELATED DOCUMENTS

This section describes documents which are not themselves deeds, but which are relevant to their evidence. The first part looks at the varied documents often found in deed bundles in addition to deeds themselves, while the remainder concerns alternative and supplementary sources of deed evidence.

THE CONTENTS OF DEED BUNDLES

The main alternative to transfer of property by sale is transfer by inheritance. Wills are therefore frequently included with title deeds. They may be the 'probate copies', on parchment with a copy of the grant of probate attached,[20] but if the will deals with more than one piece of property, then each deed bundle may contain a paper copy.

---

[20]   The record of its proof in the church court, that made the will legally valid. The original will with the grant of probate endorsed is retained among the diocesan records.

Abstracts of title also refer to wills, but they only give details about the actual bequests of property. Naturally, anyone searching for wills for family or social history will look first in diocesan or county record offices rather than deed bundles, but the latter can be helpful, particularly in locating wills proved in the Prerogative Court of Canterbury (now at the P.R.O.), for which place indexes are non-existent after 1700. It is very rare for the wills in deed bundles to have survived better than those in record offices,[21] but wills with deeds can still be of value. Firstly, the associated deeds usually clarify the relationships between the people named in the will and those in other records. Secondly, the descriptions of property in wills are often rather vague e.g. 'the house wherein I dwell', or 'my messuage and land in the parish of X'. Often the only way to locate these precisely is through the related title deeds. This can be particularly valuable in relation to *probate inventories*. These are lists of the deceased person's possessions (excluding property), which frequently accompany the wills in the dioc-esan records. They are immensely valuable for social history, particularly if they can be related to specific houses or farms. Unfortunately, the vagueness of wills generally leaves this relationship unclear, but deeds help to overcome the problem.[22]

Other documents in deed bundles are also concerned with descent. Frequently, certified copies of **baptism, marriage,** and **burial certificates** are included to give proof of relationships, and sometimes drawn-out **pedigrees** are found, when the family links are particularly complicated. **Statutory declarations** (statements made under oath following statutory requirements) may also explain family connections, though they also cover other matters. They were most commonly used if no deeds could be found, to declare that the owner had been in undisturbed possession for many years.

Deed bundles may also contain miscellanea relating to the property itself. These include **sale particulars** and **auction announcements**, which often give details about the property, numbers of rooms, tenants' names, etc., that are not in the deeds. **Insurance policies** were often kept with deeds, and the early ones have brief descriptions, particularly covering the construction and materials of houses. **Building contracts** are more informative still, though very rare.

A final group is of legal papers. These may include **counsel's opinions**, for example on the validity of a title deed. Most frequent are **solicitor's bills** for carrying out purchases. They are not generally very significant for the history either of the property or the people concerned, though contemplation of the level of costs is salutary.

COPIES OF COURT ROLL AND MANORIAL COURT ROLLS

Like the enrolled deeds described earlier (p.39), the court rolls or court books give the same information as the individual deeds, the *copies*, but their status reverses that

---

[21] Except for Devon and Somerset, where almost all the wills were destroyed in 1942. Early wills also may not survive elsewhere.

[22] See, for example, N. W. Alcock, *People at Home* (Phillimore, 1993). for a study of inventory evidence related to individual property holdings.

of the enrolled copies.[23] The court roll itself is the original authentic record, and the individual document is the copy, though it was accepted by the manor court as good evidence of title. In the medieval period, changes of tenant on most of the 15,000 manors in England were recorded on the court rolls, unless the tenant held 'at will'. This developed into the tenure known as *copy*hold, because the tenant received a *copy* of the entry on the roll to prove his tenancy; if the manor was surveyed, he was expected to produce this copy at the special manorial court of survey.

Copyhold was governed by the 'custom of the manor', which varied considerably from one manor to another. In some places, copyhold land could be inherited or bought and sold without the permission of the lord of the manor, by paying a standard fee. However, its 'owner' was still technically a tenant of the manor, and the court rolls or books therefore record changes in ownership. He also had to pay a fixed rent, other manorial dues (e.g. heriot, a fine paid on the death of the tenant, consisting of either a sum of money, or the best beast or best possession) and he had to attend the manor court. On these manors, copyhold land was effectively equivalent to freehold.

In other places by the manor custom, holdings could not be inherited, but when a tenant died, the lord could regrant it to whoever he wished for life or for the lives of two or three named people; it was a short step from this to granting it on a three-life lease (and this development frequently took place). Elsewhere, copyholdings were enfranchised, with the tenant paying a lump sum to convert his tenure to freehold, extinguishing the fixed rent (see p.81); after 1841, either the landowner or the copyholder could enfranchise copyhold land without the agreement of the other. Copyhold was finally abolished by the 1922 Law of Property Act, which enfranchised all copyholdings after 1 January 1926;[24] enfranchisement was also frequent during the 19th century.

On manors without copyhold tenure, the keeping of manor courts generally came to an end in the 17th or 18th centuries, and it is all too common for most or all of the rolls to have been lost. When copyhold persisted, the court rolls were of legal importance as the main record of land 'ownership' (as it was in effect). They were therefore generally both well-kept and well-preserved, and many copyhold manors have continuous runs from the 16th or 17th centuries until 1922. The court records are generally actual rolls until about 1700, but court books were very often adopted after that. These frequently have indexes of people, making them very convenient to search. They are an invaluable source of information about both the land and topography of the manor, and the people and families living there.

Most sets of manor court rolls are now in county record offices, but strays are frequent. An index to the location of manorial records is kept by the National Register of Archives, London, and it is always worthwhile either visiting or writing to check any manor in which one is interested, especially as the

---

[23] P.D.A. Harvey, *Manorial Records* (British Records Association, 1984) gives an excellent general survey of manorial documents, but has very little to say about copies of court roll and does not deal with their interpretation as property deeds.

[24] Establishing compensation for the value of the copyhold was under the charge of the Ministry of Agriculture. The PRO classes MAF9 and MAF20 contain records of enfranchisement for many manors, and include deeds, court rolls and evidence of ownership of manorial rights.

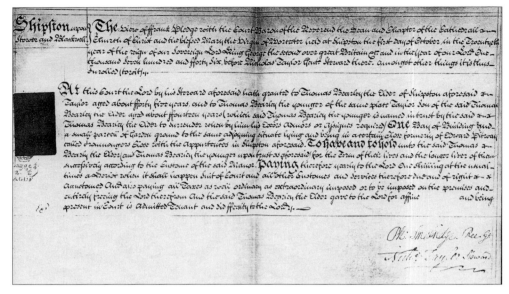

25 Eighteenth-century copy of court roll of 1746, from the manor of Shipston-upon-Stour, Warwickshire setting up a family trust for a small property in the town. For text see p.109. [SBT, ER145/5]

manorial records may be accompanied by other documents.[25] The index is good for record offices and other public collections, but it has fewer entries for rolls in private hands, and it is also incomplete for transatlantic strays. Manorial records can reasonably be expected for manors on which copyhold tenure continued to a late date (which can be established by the existence of copies of court roll). If a search of both the local record office and the Manorial Register fails, then it may be worth approaching the lord of the manor to enquire about rolls still in his hands. However, this is unlikely to be profitable for manors where copyhold tenure disappeared before the 17th or 18th century.

COPIES OF COURT ROLL

Court rolls and copies may be in Latin or English, or a mixture of the two. In post-medieval copies, the name of the manor is always at the top left, with on the right a section giving details of the court (Illus.25). A typical Warwickshire example reads:

Manor of	A Court Baron of John Knightley otherwise Wightwick, esquire, Lord of the
Berkswell	said manor, held there the second day of July in the thirty-fourth year of the
	reign of our sovereign Lord George the second, by the grace of God ...,
	Before Joseph Cater, gentleman, steward there. [1760; WRO, CR1300/6/1]

[25] Mary Ellis, *Using Manorial Records* (Public Record Office, 1994) discusses in detail the location of manorial records both in the P.R.O. and elsewhere. In theory, though not always in practice, manorial records must be kept in an approved repository (e.g. a county record office) and may not be exported without the permission of the Master of the Rolls (which has never been given).

The second part of the copy gives the details of the property and the change of ownership, as recorded on the roll. They tend to be much less wordy than ordinary deeds, and are easier to follow. The simplest form records the death of the previous owner and the admission of his heir. This was not necessarily the eldest son, as many manors had the custom of Borough English, by which the youngest son inherited. To take over the property, the heir would appear in the court and be admitted and given seizin by the steward, as in the following example. It is notable in this example that the fine is substantial, indicating that the custom on this manor was not that of inheritance for a fixed fine (usually set by custom at one or two year's rent).

> [Allesley, Warwickshire] At this court it is presented by the homage that Mary Beck the Free Bench widow of William Beck late a copyhold tenant of this manor is dead since the last court and that his nephew George Beck an infant of the age of sixteen years and upwards, the only son of John Beck deceased who was the elder brother of the said William Beck, is the next heir to the said William Beck, Whereupon at this court came the said George Beck in his proper person and prayed to be admitted tenant to the copyhold lands and tenements of which the said William Beck died seized (that is to say) to All that messuage … [*description of property totalling about one acre, including the names of former tenants*] To whom the lord of the said manor by me his steward hath granted seizin and he hath seizin thereof by the rod [*a ceremony in the court*] according to the custom of the said manor to have and to hold the same with the appurtenances to him the said George and his heirs for ever according to the custom of the said manor by the yearly rent of 8 shillings, suit of court, heriott when it shall happen and all other rents, services and customs therefore due and of right accustomed, and he gave the lord for a fine six pounds and is admitted tenant thereto accordingly, but his fealty is respited by reason of nonage [*being under age*], In witness whereof I the steward have hereunto put my hand and seal [1755; WRO, CR623/box 2].[26]

If another change of ownership was involved, then the original owner surrendered the property to the lord of the manor, but could specify the 'use' for the property. This was the feature of copyhold tenure that made it equivalent to freehold. The most straightforward case is that of the sale of the property, when the property was surrendered to the use of the purchaser, as in the following example; the surrender did not have to take place in the manor court, but could be made to two of the manorial tenants at any convenient place (e.g. the bedroom of a dying tenant).

> [Borough of Lewes, Sussex] At this court comes William Cooper, gentleman, and Elizabeth, his wife, (the said Elizabeth being first solely and secretly examined by the said Steward and consenting) [*to demonstrate that she was not being coerced into relinquishing her rights*] and surrenders into the hands of the Lords of the said borough [*the borough had joint lords*],

---

[26]   This and most of the following items are quoted from the manor court rolls and papers which provide a good range of examples of the court business. For each item, a copy of court roll would also have been prepared, but these have often not survived.

26 Memorandum of a surrender for a mortgage, for enrolment on the manor court roll of Allesley, Warwickshire. For text see p.109. [WRO CR623/box 2]

all that small parcel of land …, paying to the lords yearly 6d, To the use and behoof of John Jones of the Parish of All Saints, dyer, his heirs and assigns for ever and the said John Jones being present in Court desires to be admitted to the said premises, to whom the Lords by the steward aforesaid grant seizin thereof by the rod to have and to hold the same unto the said John Jones, his heirs and assigns for ever by copy of court roll at the will of the Lords, according to the custom of the said borough, by the rents, customs, and services therefore first due and of right accustomed, he is admitted tenant thereof paying to the Lords for a fine therefore 6d of certain [*i.e. a fine fixed by custom and not at the lord's choice*] [1733; private ownership].

Property to be left by will was surrendered while the owner was alive:

To the use and behoof of his last will and testament in writing to be declared

and when the heir came to be admitted, he would produce the will and the admission would refer to the previous surrender. This was important if the tenant had several children. If he made no will, his freehold land would pass to his eldest son, but following 'Borough English', the copyhold land would pass to the youngest son; such a division might well not be intended. It was also possible to create a family settlement, e.g. in a surrender in 1676 by Thomas Abbey of Allesley:

> To the use and behoof of the said Thomas Abbey and the said Joyce his wife for and
> dureing their naturall lives and the life of the longer liver of them, And ymediatly from and
> after the decease of the survivor of them the said Thomas Abbey and Joyce his wife, then
> to the use and behoof of ... Abbey (onely sonne of Henry Abbey, deceased and grandsonne
> of the said Thomas Abbey) and of his heirs [WRO, CR623/box2].

Copyhold land could also be mortgaged (Illus.26); it was surrendered to the use of
the mortgagee conditional on the repayment of the money due:

> [South Malling, Sussex] To the ... use of ... Walter Brett and John Savage ... [on the
> condition that] if the said Thomas Wynchester , his heires, executors, administrators or
> assigns or any of them doe at or in the nowe dwelling house of the said Walter Brett situat
> in Lewes in the county of Sussex well and truly cause to be paid to the said Walter and John,
> their heirs, [etc.] ..., being both present in person, the some of two hundred and six pounds
> of lawful money in and upon the 3 and 20th day of October next, this surrender to be void
> or else to remain in force [1654] [*Margin*] Memorandum that the moneys in the condicion
> mentioned was payd according to the tenor of the condicion] [British Library, Add. Mss.
> 33183].

It was even possible to carry out a Common Recovery in the manor court, so that
property which had been included in a family settlement could be sold or re-settled.
The steward certainly would have needed very careful guidance in just how this was
done, as shown in Illustration 27.

MANORIAL CUSTOMS

Some items in the court rolls relate directly to the customs of the manor. The tenant
of a copyholding might not always be allowed to sub-lease the property, because the
sub-tenant would not have the same responsibility towards the other tenants as the
copyholder himself; he would therefore need 'liberty of licence' to sub-lease, and
would agree that the lord could distrain on the tenement if the rents and services due
were not paid as required.

The widow of a copyholder was permitted to continue to hold the tenement after
his death, as her 'Free Bench' (as with Mary Beck, above), until her death or remarriage.
Much more rarely, a widower might have free bench in the tenement his wife had held
in her own right.[27] The custom of free bench was sometimes turned to the tenant's
advantage on manors where copyhold land was not automatically inherited. An elderly
tenant would marry a young woman, who might retain the holding for many years after
his death. She would be in an excellent position to bargain for a renewal of the
copyhold on advantageous terms, for the benefit of her husband's children. Of course,
such schemes might misfire—in one case in 1620, the tenant was rejuvenated by his
marriage and survived for another 15 years![28] Surprisingly, the customs of the manor
might also relate to morals and behaviour, though this was normally only the concern

---

[27] For example, in Temple Balsall, Warwickshire in 1655; Warwick Record Office, CR112/412.
[28] See J.H. Bettey, 'Manorial customs and widows' estate', *Archives*, 19 (1987), 208-16.

APPENDIX.

The Form of suffering a Recovery in a Manor-Court, ought to be in the following manner :—

A. B. is the tenant in tail, and desirous of barring the entail by a recovery. In this case *C. D.* must be made tenant to the plaint, or tenant to the precipe ; and *E. F.* as demandant, is to bring his action against *C. D.* for the lands. *A. B.* then comes in as vouchee, to vouch over *R. M.* the common voucher of the court. The copyholds must in the first place be surrendered to the use of *C. D.* : to make him tenant to the plaint, and he must be admitted in the usual manner ; the steward then addressing himself to *E. F.* the demandant : " You being now in court, in " your own proper person, complain against " *C. D.* tenant to the plaint, of a plea of land, " to wit, one messuage, one curtilage, &c. hol- " den of this manor by copy of court-roll, at " the will of the lord ; and therefore you pray " process to be awarded against him ; but you " the said *C. D.* voluntarily appear to answer " to the said *E. F.* and thereupon you, the said " *E. F.* demand against the said *C. D.* the te- " nements aforesaid, with the appurtenances, as " your right and inheritance, and say that you " were seised of the same, in your demesne, as " of fee and right, according to the custom of " this manor, at the will of the lord, and into " which the said *C. D.* has not entry but after

" the

APPENDIX.

" the disseisin of one *Hugh Hunt* ; whereup- " on you *C. D.* come and defend your right to " the tenements aforesaid, with the appurte- " nances, and vouch over to warranty *A. B.* " to which you *A. B.* appear. And thereup- " on you *E. F.* make the like demand against " the said *A. B.* as against the said *C. D.* and " say that you were seised of the tenements afore- " said, with the appurtenances, in your de- " mesne, as of fee and right, according to the " custom of this manor, at the will of the lord, " and into which the said *A B.* has not entry, " but after the disseisin of the said *Hugh Hunt* ; " whereupon you *A. B.* come and defend this " right of the said *C. D.* to the tenement afore- " said, with the appurtenances, and further call " to warranty *Ralph May* ; and thereupon, you " *E. F.* make the like demand against the " said *Ralph May* as against the said *A. B.* " and say that you was seised of the tenements " aforesaid, with the appurtenances in your " demesne, as of fee and right, according to the " custom of the manor, at the will of the lord ; " and into which the said *Ralph May* has not " entry, but after the disseisin of the said " *Hugh Hunt* ; whereupon you, *Ralph May,* " come and defend the right of the said *C. D.* " and say, that the said *Hugh Hunt* did not " disseise the said *E. F.* of the tenement afore- " said, as the said *E. F.* does by his plaint above " pretend and allege ; and thereupon you, *E. F.*

---

27   Instructions for a manor court steward to carry out a Common Recovery of copyhold land. From Richard Barnard Fisher, *A practical treatise on copyhold tenure* (London, 1803). The instructions continue with the leave to imparle, the failure of Ralph May, the common vouchee, to return, the judgement for E. F., and the precept of the court to the bailiff to deliver seizin to E. F. This is followed by the seven-page text of the recovery as it is to be entered on the court roll.

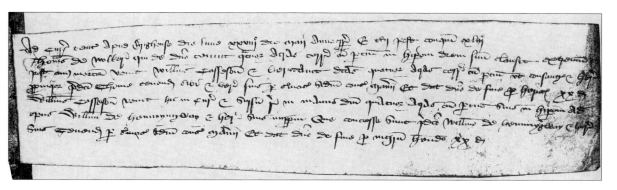

28   Fourteenth-century copy of court roll of 1369, from the manor of Wakefield, Yorkshire. For text see p.110. [Yorkshire Archaeological Society, Leeds, Foster-Greenwood Collection, DD99/A3/4]

of the Church Courts. In 1633, in Temple Balsall, Warwickshire, it was recorded that Margery Findern who was with child before her marriage with Henry Essex had forfeited all right in her copyhold lands according to the custom of the manor, but she was able to redeem these by bringing in a purse worth 1d. (*unum crumenam ad valenciam unius denarius*) and 5s. in money, and was readmitted.

Medieval Copies of Court Roll

Medieval copies are very rare though this seems not simply to be a matter of survival; the reasons why some manors but not others produced them have yet to be explored.[29] Illustration 28 shows a 14th-century example; it is notable that it includes many of the key features of copyhold, particularly its 'surrender to uses', for the benefit of a named person and the payment of a standard fine. Such features begin to appear as early as the beginning of the 14th century, especially in East Anglia, but the systematic development of copyhold tenure into its full post-medieval form took place mainly in the 15th century.[30] By the 16th to 17th centuries the entries on the court rolls were following the standard later forms.

It is also worth noting that medieval court rolls can give information about freeholdings, because manorial custom often required a 'relief' (e.g. 5s) to be paid when a freeholding was transferred, and the payment of (or failure to pay) these reliefs would be recorded in the court rolls. This has been used effectively, for example, in the manor of Wrotham, Kent, to show that the builders of its handsome late medieval timber-framed houses were often butchers, tanners or others involved

[29]   Harvey, *op. cit.* in n.35, p.44, notes very early references to copies of court roll from 1311 and 1315. Among manors for which I have encountered medieval copies are Harringey, Middlesex (see P.R.O. Descriptive Catalogue of Ancient Deeds, H.M.S.O. 1915, vol.6, indexed under 'manor courts'); Sedgley, Staffordshire (in Staffordshire Record Office), and Wakefield, West Yorkshire (in West Yorkshire Record Office).

[30]   Professor C. Dyer has noted surrenders in early 14th-century rolls of Blickling, Norfolk [Norfolk Record Office] for the use of a named person, with the condition that they would be void unless specified sums of money were paid; these probably represent deferred purchase payments rather than loans of money (personal communication). For the 15th-century development of copyhold, see E.B. Fryde and N. Fryde, in Edward Miller (ed.), *Ag. Hist. III: 1348-1500* (Cambridge, 1991), p.813f.

in the London meat trade.[31] Thus, even on non-copyhold manors, the medieval court rolls (if they survive) can give invaluable information about tenants and land owners and their property.

The translation of the medieval copy of court roll from Wakefield (Illus.28, text on p.110) shows the similarity in its content to later copies.

> At the court held at Brighouse on Monday 28th May in the 43rd year of the reign of Edward the third after the conquest [1369], [presented that, *understood*] Thomas de Wolker who held of the lord four acres of land with appurtenances in Hiperom [Hipperholme, Wakefield] died [*closed his last day*], after whose death came William Casseson and inherited the said four acres of land with appurtenances as kinsman and next heir of the said Thomas, to hold to him and his heirs by the services [*due*] according to the customs of the manor. And he gives the lord for a fine. 20d. William Casseson came here in court and surrendered into the lord's hand the four acres with its appurtenances in Hiperom, to the use of William de Hemmyngway and his heirs for ever, Which were granted to the aforesaid William de Hemmyngway and his heirs to hold by the service [*due*] according to the customs of the manor. And he gives the lord for a fine to have entry, 20d.

---

[31] Unpublished study by Jayne Semple.

Texts of Deeds

1. Texts of illustrated deeds

1. Thirteenth-century lease of a house in Coventry (p.3)

Sciant presentes et futuri quod ego Robertus de Feug's tradidi ad firmam Galfridi de Wilnhall, domum meam inter pontes in Covintr', in qua manere consuevi, scilicet domum illam propinquior aque, cum pertinentiis suis, habendam et tenendam de me et de heredibus meis, sibi et heredibus suis libere et quiete et honorifice, a Nativitate Sancti Johannis Baptiste tercia post translationem Beati Thome martiris, usque ad decem annos sequentes completos, pro quattuor marcis argenti, quas ipse Galfridi michi dedit, scilicet totam firmam decem annorum pre manibus. Et ego Robertus et heredes mei warantizabimus predicto Galfrido et heredibus suis predictam domum cum pertinentiis suis per decem annos contra omnes homines et omnes feminas. Et totum servitium quod debetur capitalibus dominis de domo illa singulis annis adquietabimus. Completis vero decem annis predicta domus cum pertinentiis suis remanebit michi et heredibus meis sola et quieta ab ipso Galfrido et ab omnibus suis sine omni contradictione. Hanc autem conventionem legaliter et sine dolo tenendam utrimque affidavimus. In cuius rei testimonium presenti scripto sigillum meum apposui. Hiis testibus Willelmo filio Umfredi, Johanne filio eius, Swano parcario, Vincentio filio eius, Henrico filio Edredi, Willelmo de Franketon, Thoma tinctore, Hamone filio Jordani, Roger de Cornl', Roberto Blundo, Michaele tinctore, et aliis.

TRANSLATION:
Know all men present and future that I Robert de Feugers [*a name known from other documents*] have leased at farm [*for a money rent*] to Geoffrey de Willenhall, my house between the bridges [*in a street later called Burges*] in Coventry, in which I have been accustomed to dwell, to wit that house beside the water, with its appurtenances, to have and to hold of me and of my heirs, to him and his heirs freely, both quietly and honorably, from the [*feast of the*] Birth of Saint John the Baptist [*24 June*], the third after the Translation of the Blessed Thomas [*a Becket*] martyr [*as the translation took place on 7th July 1220, the date indicated is 24 June 1223*] for ten years following to be completed, for four marks of silver, which the same Geoffrey gave me, to wit the whole farm of ten years in advance. And I, Robert, and my heirs warrant to the said Geoffrey and his heirs, the said house with its appurtenances for ten years

against all men and all women. And all service which is owed to the chief lord from that house for every single year we will acquit. Indeed, on completion of the ten years the said house with its appurtenances shall remain to me and my heirs solely and quietly from the said Geoffrey and from all of his [heirs] without any gainsaying. Moreover, we pledge ourselves to hold this agreement legally and without fraud. In witness whereof I have affixed my seal to this present charter. These being witnesses: William son of Humphrey, John his son, Swain the parker, Vincent his son, Henry son of Edred, William de Franketon, Thomas the dyer, Hamon son of Jordan, Roger de Corley, Robert Blund, Michael the dyer, and others.

17. SEVENTEENTH-CENTURY LEASE (OF A LEASE AND RELEASE) FOR AVON DASSETT, WARWICKSHIRE (P.62)

This indenture made the nine and twentyth day of May Anno Domini one thousand six hundred and eighty and in the two and thirtyeth year of the reigne of our Soveraigne Lord Charles the Second by the grace of God, of England, Scotland, Fraunce and Ireland, kinge, defender of the faith, etc. BETWEENE William Rose of Walton in the parish of Wellesborne in the County of Warwicke, yeoman of the one part, and John Vennor of Wellesborne Mountford in the said County, gentleman, Thomas Goodwyn the younger of Binton in the said County, yeoman, and Edward Atwood of Newnham in the parish of Aston Cantelowe in the said County, yeoman, and Mary Atwood his daughter, of the other part, WITNESSETH that the said William Rose for and in consideration of the summe of five shillings of lawful money to him in hand paid by the said John Vennor and Thomas Goodwyn the younger, the receipte whereof the said William Rose doth hereby acknowledge and thereof acquitt and dischardge the said John Vennor and Thomas Goodwyn, their heirs, executors and administrators and every of them, and for other good causes and considerations him the said William Rose thereunto moveing HATH bargained, sold, demysed and to farme letten And by theese presents doth bargaine, sell, demise and to farm lett unto the said John Vennor and Thomas Goodwyn, their executors, administrators and assigns, ALL that his messuage or tenement with appurtenances scituate and being in Avon Dassett in the said County of Warwicke and all that his halfe yard lande of arrable, meadowe and pasture ground wuth their appurtenances, lyeinge and beinge dispersed in the open and common fieldes of Avon Dassett aforesaid, Togeather with all and singular howses, outhowses, buildinges, barnes, stables, Cow yardes, backsides, orchards, gardens, landes, leyes, hades, bawlkes, furrowes, meadow grounde, lott ground, trees, woods, underwoods, furze, thornes, lott furze and thornes, commons and common of pasture, wayes, waters, passages, profitts, comodities, advantages, hereditaments and appurtenances to the said messuage and halfe yard land and other the premisses belonginge or in any wise appertaninge or therewith used or enioyed or reputed or taken as parte, parcell or member thereof And the revercion and revercions, remaynder and remaynders, rents and services of the premisses and of evry part thereof, TO HAVE AND TO HOULD the said messuage or tenemente halfe yard land and other the premisses with appurtenances unto the said John Vennor and Thomas Goodwyn, their executors administrators and assigns, to the use of them, their executors administrators and assigns for and dureing and unto the full end and terme of one whole yeare from the first day of this instant moneth of May thence next and ymediately ensueing and fully to be compleate and ended, TO the intente that by vertue heereof and by force of the Statute for transferringe of uses into possession, the said John Vennor and Thomas Goodwyn may be enabled to take and accepte of a release of all and singuler the said messuage or tenemente, halfe yard land and premisses to them, their heirs and assigns, IN WITNESS whereof the partyes first above named to theis presente indentures have interchaungably putt to their handes and seales the day and year above written.

Thomas Goodwin Edward Allwood

18. Seventeenth-century terrier of open-field land in Thurlaston, Warwickshire attached to a deed of 1616 (p.66)

A trewe and perfecte Terrur containeinge the dwellinge howse, with thappurtennces, and all the landes, leyes, meadowe and pasture of one Henrie Bromfeild of Thurleston in the countie of Warr' yeoman, belongeinge unto or occupied with the said dwelling howse, and all comons for beasse, sheepe and horses accordinge to the scale and stinte of the same lande examined and allowed by the steward and homage theire att the courte then holden the seventh daie of October in the yeare of the raigne of our soveraigne lorde James the kinges majestie that now ys of England the seventh and of Scotland the xliiith 1609.

Inprimis the foresaid dwellinge howse, one yard land, threescore sheepe common, eight beasse comons, foure horses or mares & one breeder, one closse, one orchard, one garden adioyninge to the said howse next the comon of Thurleston of thone side and one Thomas Smyth of thother side

The East Feylde or Breach Feylde

Item one Roode lyeinge one [on] Breach Furlonge buttinge into London Waie and to Cawson Hedge betwene the land in the occupacion of Roberte Atkins on the east side & the land in the occupacion of Elizabeth Bucknoll, widdowe on the west side.

Item one other lande lyeinge on the same furlonge buttinge into London Waye betwene Thomas Smyth of the easte side and the land in the occupacion of Richard Sale of the west side

Item five roodes lyeinge on Crosse Furlonge buttinge into London waye betwene Thomas Smyth of the east side and the land in the occupacion of Richard Sale of the west side

Item one other land lyeinge on the same furlonge buttinge into London waie betwen the land in the occupacion of John Guppill of the easte side and the land in the occupacion of Elizabeth Bucknoll of the weste side

 Item one acre on Little Crosse Furlonge lyeinge betwene the lande of Thomas Marris on the south side and the lande in the occupacion of Elizabeth Bucknoll on the [south, *erased*] north side

19. Seventeenth-century bond relating to the bequest of a stable in Greyfriar Lane, Coventry (p.71)

[First portion in Latin:] Noverint universi per presentes me Joan Meare de Civitatis Coventrie, spinster, teneri et firmiter obligari Samueli Tissele, senior, de Civitatis predicti, clothier, in sexaginta libris bonae et legalis monetae Angliae, solvendis eidem Samueli Tissele aut suo certo attornato executoribus vel administratoribus suis, ad quam quidem solucionem bene et fideliter faciendam, obligo me, heredes, executores et administratores meos firmiter per presentes sigillo meo sigillati, dato sexto die Octobris annoque domini 1688.

Translation:
Know all by these presents, that I, Joan Meare of Coventry, spinster, am bound and firmly obliged to Samuel Tissele, senior of Coventry, clothier, in sixty pounds of good and legal money of England, to pay the same Samuel Tissele or his certain attorney, his executors or administrators, to well and faithfully making of which payment, I firmly bind myself, my heirs, executors and administrators by these presents, sealed with my seal, Given the sixth day of October [*regnal year omitted*] and in the year of our Lord 1688.

[continues as follows]
The condition of this obligacion is such whereas the above bounden Joane Meere hath the day of the date hereof made and ordained her last will and testament, and hath therein given and bequeathed to her kinswoman Susanna Broadstreet after her decease, one stable in Grayfryer Lane, as therein and thereby is limited, appaynted [*appointed*] and declared, together alsoe with her personal estate whatsoever, as relacion thereunto had may more fully appear, if therfore the said Joan Meere above bounden doe from time to time and at all times hereafter stand to and abide by the said will, and make noe other will or alteration therein, then this obligacion to be void or else remain in full force. Sealed and delivered in the Presence of

Joan Meare John Thompson, Joan Rock [R] her mark, John Brockhurst [*text and the subscription of Joan Rock in the hand of John Brockhurst, presumably the lawyer*]

20. Seventeenth-century final concord ('Fine') for a messuage in Coventry (p.74)

Hec est finalis concordia facta in curia domini Regis apud Westmonasterium in Octavis Sancti Hilarii Anno Regnorum Jacobi Dei gratia Angli Scotie Francie et Hibernie Regis fidei defensoris etc, Angli Francie et Hibernie undecimo et Scotie quadragesimo septimo, coram Henrici Hobarte, Petro Warburton, Humfrido Winche et Augustino Nicolls justiciariis et aliis domino Regis fidelibus tunc ibi presentibus, Inter Willelmus Wightwicke querens et Thomam Kildermer et Margeriam uxorem eius deforciantes de uno mesuagio uno gardino et uno pomario cum pertinentiis in parochia Sancti Michaelis unde placitum convencionis summonitum fuit inter eos in eadem curia, Scilicet quod predicti Thomas et Margeria recognoverunt predictam tenementam cum pertinentiis esse ius ipsius Willelmi ut illud que idem Willelmus habebit de dono predictorum Thome et Margerie et illi remiserunt et quietclamaverunt de ipsis Thoma et Margeria et heredibus suis predicto Willelmo et heredibus suis in perpetuum, Et preterea iidem Thomas et Margeria concesserunt pro se et heredes ipsius Thome quod ipsi warantizabunt predicto Willelmo et heredibus suis predictam tenementam cum pertinentiis contra predictos Thomam et Margeriam et heredes ipsius Thome in perpetuum, Et pro hac recognitione remissione quietclamatione warantia fine et concordia, idem Willelmus dedit predictis Thome et Margerie quadraginta et unam libras sterlingorum.

Translation:
This is the final agreement made in the court of the lord king at Westminster in the octave of St Hilary [*i.e. the spring Law Term, starting on 20th January, a week after the saint's feast*] in the year of the reign of James by the grace of God King of England, Scotland, France, and Ireland, defender of the faith, etc., of England France and Ireland the eleventh, and of Scotland the fortyseventh [*1614*], before Henry Hobarte, Peter Warburton, Humphrey Winche, and Augustine Nicolls, justices, and other faithful (subjects) of the lord King there then present, Between William Wightwicke, plaintiff; and Thomas Kildermer and Margery his wife, defendants, of one messuage, one garden, and one orchard with their appurtenances in the parish of St Michael [*Coventry*], concerning which a plea of covenant was summoned between them in the same court, To wit that the said Thomas and Margery have recognised that the said tenement with its appurtenances is of the right of of the same William, as that which the same William had of the gift of the said Thomas and Margery, and they remise and quitclaim for the same Thomas and Margery and their heirs to the said Williamm and his heirs for ever, And further, the same Thomas and Margery grant for them and the heirs of the same Thomas that they will warrant the said tenement with its appurtenances to the said William and his heirs against the said Thomas and Margery and the heirs of the same Thomas for ever, and for this acknowledgment, remission, quitclaim, warranty, fine, and agreement, the same William gave the said Thomas and Margery forty-one pounds sterling.

23. FIFTEENTH-CENTURY LETTER OF ATTORNEY (P.85)

Noverint universi per presentes me dominum Johannem Bewchamp militem attornasse et loco meo apposuisse dilectos mihi in Christo Johannem Wilde capitale ballivum meum de Alcestr' ac Thomam Freston et Rogerum Smythe sub-ballivos de eadem in veros et legittimos attornatos ad deliberandum Thome Madley de Alcestre, bocher, plenam et pacificam pocessionem de et in una parcella terre condam [*quondam*] vacua et nunc per ipsum Thomam de novo edificata in Colbroke in villa de Alcestr' infra comitatum Warwick', habendum et tenendum predictam parcellam terre cum pertinenciis predicto Thome, et Agnete uxori eius et heredibus inter predictos Thomam et Agnetem legittime procreatis iuxta vim formam et effectam quarundam indenturarum inter prefatum dominum et dictum Thomam inde confectarum. Ratum habiturum et gratum, quicquid iidem attornati mei aut duo eorum fecerint in premissis sicut ego prefatus dominus personaliter interessem proviso semper quod dictus capitalis ballivus meus sit unus illorum duorum. In cuius rei testimonium huic scripto meo atornati sigillum meum aposui. Datum apud Alcestre predicto, tercio die mencis Septembris anno regni regis Edwardi quarti post conquestum duodecimo.

TRANSLATION

Know all men by these presents that I Lord John Bewchamp, knight, attourn and in my place appoint the beloved to me in Christ John Wilde, my chief bailiff of Alcester, and Thomas Freston and Roger Smythe, sub-bailiffs of the same, my true and legitimate attorneys to deliver to Thomas Madley of Alcester, butcher, full and peaceable possession of and in one parcel of formerly vacant land, now newly built on by the same Thomas in Colbroke in the town of Alcester within the county of Warwick, to have and to hold the said parcel of land, to the same Thomas, Agnes his wife, and the heirs of the said Thomas and Agnes between them legitimately begotten, following the form and effect of certain indentures between the said lord and the said Thomas, made. And that I will hold as accepted and agreed whatsoever those my attorneys or two of them shall do in this matter as if I the said lord were present in person provided always that my said chief bailiff shall be one of those two. In witness whereof, I have affixed my seal to this my writing of attorney, dated at Alcester aforesaid, the third day of the month of September in the 12th year of the reign of King Edward the fourth after the conquest [1472].

24. MEDIEVAL GIFT: SEE PAGE 86.

25. Eighteenth-century copy of court roll. (p.96)

Shipston upon Stower and Blackwell [Warwickshire] The view of Frank Pledge with the Court Baron of the Reverend the Dean and Chapter of the Cathedrall Church of Christ and the blessed Mary the Virgin of Worcester, held at Shipston the first day of October in the Twentyeth year of the reign of our Sovereign Lord King George the second over great Britain etc and in the Year of our Lord One thousand Seven hundred and Forty six, before Nicholas Taylor Gent, Steward there, amongs other things it is thus Inrolled (to wit):

At this Court the Lord by his Steward aforesaid hath granted to Thomas Bearley the elder of Shipston aforesaid, Taylor, aged about forty five years, and to Thomas Bearley the younger of the same place, Taylor, Son of the said Thomas Bearley the Elder, aged about fourteen years (which said Thomas Bearley the younger is named in trust by the said Thomas Bearley the Elder, to surrender when by him, his executors, administrators, or assignes required) One Bay of Building and a small parcell of Garden ground to the same adjoyning, situate, lying and being in a certain Close formerly of Edward Pitway, called Ironmongers Close, with the Appurtenances in Shipston aforesaid, To have and to hold unto the said Thomas Bearley the Elder (and Thomas Bearley the younger upon trust as aforesaid) for the Term of their lives and the longer liver of them successively according to the Custome of the said Manor, Paying therefore yearly to the Lord one shilling at the usual times, a Heriot when it shall happen, Suit of Court and all other Customes and Services therefore due and of right Accustomed, And also paying all Taxes as well ordinary as extraordinary imposed or to be imposed on the premises, and entirely freeing the Lord therefrom, And the said Thomas Bearley the Elder gave to the Lord for a fine [*blank*] and being present in Court is admitted Tenant and did Fealty to the Lord. [*Signed by the Receiver General of the Dean and Chapter and the Steward*]

26. Eighteenth-century memorandum for enrolment on the manor court roll of Allesley, Warwickshire (p.98)

Manor of Allesley. Memorandum that on the eleventh day of August in the twenty third year of the Reign of our Sovereign Lord George the second by the Grace of God of Great Britain, France and Ireland King, Defender of the Faith and so forth and in the year of our Lord One thousand seven hundred and forty nine, Samuel Crichlowe of the City of Coventry, Wollen Draper, one of the Customary Tennants of the Manor aforesaid and Alley his wife (the said Alley being first secretly Examined by James Birch, Gentleman, Steward there and thereto consenting) Did out of Court according to the Custome of the said Manor and hereby Doe surrender by the Rod into the hands of the Lord of the said Manor by the Hands of the said James Birch, All those Customary Messuages, Lands, Tenements and Hereditaments with the appurtenances scituate, lying and being in Allesley aforesaid, being part of

the Copyhold Tenements of the said Manor and now or late in the occupation of
Thomas Rowe and Joanna Jefferys or one of them, their or one of their assignee
or assigns, To the use and behoof of William Gilbert of the City of Coventry
aforesaid, Tammy Merchant, his heirs and assigns for ever according to the custom
of the said Manor by the Rents and services therefore Due and of Right accustomed, Provided always nevertheless and upon this condition that if the said Samuel
Crichlowe his heirs, executors or administrators do and shall well and truly pay or
cause to be paid unto the said William Gilbert, his executors, administrators or
assigns, the full and just sum of four hundred and eight pounds of lawfull money
of Great Britain upon the nineth day of February next without any Deduction or
abatement whatsoever for and on account of Taxes or otherwise howsoever, That
then this surrender shall be Void and of none Effect or else to be and remain in
full force and Virtue.   [signed] Sam Crichlowe
This surrender was duly taken and Alley Crichlowe acknowledged before me
[signed] Ja Birch known & Steward of the said Manor

28.   FOURTEENTH-CENTURY COPY OF COURT ROLL FROM THE MANOR OF
             WAKEFIELD (p.101)[For translation, see p.102]

Ad curiam tentam apud Brighouse die lune xxviij° die Maii anno regni regis
Edwardi tertii post conquestum xliij°, Thomas de Wolker qui de domino tenuit
quatuor acras terre cum pertinentiis in Hiperom diem suum clausit extremum. Post
cuius mortem venit Willelmus Casseson et heriotavit dictas quatuor acras terre cum
pertinentiis ut consanguineus et heres propinquior predicti Thome, tenendas sibi et
heredibus suis per servicio secundum consuetudinem manerii, Et dat domino de
fine pro herietis xxd. Willelmus Casseson venit hic in curia et sursum reddidit in
manus domini quatuor acras cum pertinentiis suis in Hiperom, ad opus Willelmi de
Hemmyngway et heredibus suis in perpetuum, Que concesse sunt predicto Willelmo
de Hemmyngway et heredibus suis tenende per serviciis secundum consuetudinem
manerii. Et dat domino de fine pro ingressu habendo xxd.

2. Example of a release

Seventeenth-century release (of a lease and release)
[Introduction and date] This indenture made the sixteenth day of March in the
thirtyeth yeare of the raigne of our Sovereign Lord Charles the Second by the grace
of God, of England, Scotland, France and Ireland, Kinge, defender of the faith, etc.
annoque domini 1677
[Parties] BETWEENE Samuell Hope of the Citty of Coventry in the county of the
same city, tayler, Richard Palmer of the Citty of Coventry aforesaid, tayler, and Mary
his wife, and Hanna Hope of the Citty of Coventry aforesaid, spinster, sisters of the

said Samuell Hope of the one part, and Michael Mann of Tamworth in the county of Warwicke, clothworker, of the other part WITNESSETH that they the said Samuell Hope, Richard Palmer and Mary his wife, and Hannah Hope [*Consideration*] for and in consideration of the summe of seaven and twenty pounds of good and lawfull money of England, to them or one of them well and truely in hand paid by the said Michaell Mann before the ensealinge and delivery of these presents

[*Action*] HAVE and every of them hath graunted, bargained, sold, alyened, released, and confirmed, and by these presents doe and every of them doth graunte, bargaine, sell, alyen, releas, and confirm unto the said Michaell Mann, his heires and assigns

[*Property*: *The detailed property clause of this deed is given on page 67; it continues as follows*] With all houses, edifices, buildings, shopps, entryes, watercourses, profitts, and commodities whatsoever thereunto belonging or appurteyninge, and the revercion and revercions, remainder and remainders, of all and singuler the premisses, and all the estate, right, tytle, use, interest, possession, clayme, and demaunde whatsoever of them the said Samuell Hope, Richard Palmer and Mary his wife, and the said Hanna Hope and of every and either of them, of, in, and to the same premisses and every part thereof with the appurtenances

[*Recital of the preceding lease*] all which said premisses with the appurtenances were by them the said Samuell Hope, Richard Palmer and Mary his wife, and the said Hanna Hope for the better execution of these presents by their indenture of lease by them duely executed and beareinge date the day next before the day of the date of these presents for the considerations therein mentioned, graunted, bargained and sold unto the said Michaell Mann, his executors, administrators, and assigns for the term of six months from thence next ensueing and followinge fully to bee compleate and ended att and under the rent of one peppercorne only payable att or upon the feast of St Michaell the Archangell next ensueinge the date thereof, as in and by the said recited indenture relacion beinge thereunto had, itt may more att large appeare

[*Term, uses and tenure*] TO HAVE AND TO HOLD the said messuage or tenement and premisses hereby graunted and released with theire and every of theire appurtenances unto the said Michaell Mann, his heires and assignes for ever, to the only proper and absolute use and behoofe of the said Michaell Mann and of his heires and assigns for ever, To be held of the cheife Lord or Lords of the fee or fees of the aforesaid premises by the rents and services therefore heretofore due and of right accustomed

[*Covenant of good title*] AND the said Samuell Hope for himselfe, his heires and assignes and every of them doth covenaunte and graunt to and with the said Michaell Mann, his heires and assignes and every of them by these presents, that hee the said Samuell Hope att the time of the ensealeinge and delivery of these presents for and notwithstandinge any act or thinge by him the saide Samuell Hope or by the said Thomas Hope, father of the said Samuell Hope (party to these presents) or either of them doth to the contrary hereafter, hee the said Samuell Hope now is and standeth lawfully rightfully and absolutely seized of

and in the aforesaid messuage or tenement and premisses with theire and every
of their appurtenances and of and in every part and parcell thereof, of a good,
sure, perfect, lawfull, absolute and indefeizable estate of inheritance in fee simple
or fee tayle generall, without any manner of condicion, mortgage, or limitation
of use or uses, or other matter or thinge whatsoever to alter, change, charge,
incumber, determine, or make void the same estate

[*Of authority to make the grant*] And that he the said Samuell Hope att the time
ofthe ensealinge and delivery of these presents for and notwithstandinge any act,
matter or thinge, charge or incumbrance whatsoever by him the said Samuell Hope
or by the said Thomas Hope done to the contrary hereof, hee the said Samuell
Hope hath good right, full power, and lawfull authority in his owne righte to
graunt, bargaine, sell, releas, and confirm the hereinbefore graunted and released
premisses with theire and every of theire appurtenances, unto the said Michael
Mann, his heires and assignes for ever

[*Of quiet enjoyment*] And that he the said Michaell Mann his heires and assigns
shall and may from time to time and att all times hereafter have, hold, use,
occupie, possesse, and enjoy the said messuage or tenement and premisses with
theire and every of theire appurtenances, and receive and take the rents, issues,
and profitts thereof and of every part thereof, free and cleere and freely and
cleerely acquitted, exonerated and discharged, or from time to time and att all
times hereafter upon reasonable request well and sufficiently to bee saved, kept
harmelesse, and indempnified by he said Samuell Hope, his heires and assignes
off and from all and all manner of former and other guifts, graunts, bargaines,
sales, leases, estates, joyntures, dower, tytles, and tytle of dower, uses, wills, intayles,
rents charge, rents secke, arrearages of rent and rents, Statutes Merchant and of
the Staple, recognizances, fines, issues, amerciamentes, seizures, judgments, ex-
ecutions, and of and from all other charges, tytles, troubles, incumbrances and
demands whatsoever, had, made, committed, done or suffered to bee done or
hereafter to bee had, made, committed, done or sufferred to bee done by him
the said Samuell Hope, his heires or assignes or by the said Thomas Hope, his
heires or assignes or any of them, or by any other person claymeing by from
or under theire or either of their right tytles or interests

[*To levy a fine*] AND they the said Samuell Hope, Richard Palmer [Mary
Palmer's name was erased here), and the said Hannah Hope for themselves, theire
heires and assignes and every of them jointly and severally do convenaunte, promise
and graunt to and with the said Michaell Mann his heires and assignes and every
of them by these presents, That they the said Samuell Hope, Richard Palmer and
Mary his wife, and the said Hanna Hope shall and wilt before the end of Easter
Terme next ensueing the date hereof acknowledge and levy unto the said Michaell
Mann his heires and assignes in due forme of law one Fine *sur Cognizance de Droit
come ceo* etc. with proclamations to be thereupon had according to the forme of the
Statute in that case made and provided, Of the said messuage or tenement and all
and singuler ther the premisses with the appurtenances as by the said Michaell

Mann, his heires or assigns or his or theire councell learned in the law shall be reasonably devised or advised and required and att the proper costs and charges in the law of the said Michael Mann, his heires or assignes, Which said fine soe as aforesaid intended to bee levyed of the aforesaid premises shall bee and enure and shalbe adjudged, deemed, consstrained and taken to bee and to enure to the only proper and absolute and behoofe of the said Michaell Mann, his heires and assignes for ever, and to or for noe other use, intent or purpose whatsoever

[*Witness*] IN WITNESS whereof the parties first above named to these present indentures have interchangeably sett their hands and seales the day and yeare first above written.

Samuell Hope
The mark of Richard Palmer
The mark of Mary Palmer
The marke of Hanna Hope

[Endorsed with a receipt for the purchase price and with two
notes witnessing the signing and sealing] [private ownership]

SAMPLE DEED RECORD SHEET

Document Reference: Abstractor: Abstract No: Indexed:[   ]

Document Type (ring): Lease, Assignment, Lease and Release, Feoffment, Mortgage, Mortgage Assignment, Fine, Recovery, Settlement, other (state which)

Date (a) as in document: (b) modern style

Names of parties, occupations, abodes, relationships (Surnames as spelt, Christian names may be modernised):
1)
2)

Nature of transaction (e.g. conveyance by (1) to (3) (4) as dower trustee, (2) holds mortgage, assigned to (5) to attend inheritance)

Recitals (dates; details if not already known) (Refer to abstract sheets for earlier deeds as appropriate.):

Consideration:

Property, including abuttals and all details given:

Term (years/lives/for ever):
Rent:

Tenure and Uses:

Covenants or Conditions:

Endorsements:

ALPHABET OF POST-MEDIEVAL LETTER FORMS

Alphabet of post-medieval letter forms [from A. Wright, Court Hand Restored, (1818), originally reproduced in H.E. Grieve, *Examples of English Handwriting* (Essex Record Office, 1954). Copies of this book are available from the E.R.O.]

115

Further Information

GUIDES TO DEEDS

J. Cornwall, *An Introduction to Reading Old Title Deeds* (Federation of Family History Societies, 1997)

A.A. Dibben, *Title Deeds, 13th-19th centuries* (Historical Association, 1990)

A. Foster, 'Conveyancing Practice from Local Records', *Thoresby Society*, vol.12 (1948), p.197

C.A.F. Meekings and P. Shearman (eds.), 'Fitznell's Cartulary', *Surrey Record Society*, vol. 26 (1968)

R.B. Pugh (ed.), 'A Calendar of Antrobus Deeds to 1624', *Wiltshire Record Society*, vol.3 (1947)

LAW AND LEGAL HISTORY

W.S. Holdsworth, *An Historical Introduction to the Land Law* (Oxford University Press, 1935)

G. Jacob, *New Law Dictionary* (1729 and later editions)

F.C. Jones, *Attorney's Pocket Book* (1841)

F. Pollock, *The Land Laws* (Macmillan, 1883 and later editions)

PALAEOGRAPHY

H.E. Grieve, *Examples of English Handwriting, 1150-1750* (Essex Record Office, 1954 and later editions)

L.C. Hector, *The Handwriting of English Documents* (reprinted Kohler and Coombes, 1980)

Alf Ison, *A Secretary Hand ABC Book*, Berkshire Books, 1982 (obtainable from Berkshire Record Office). The best short guide to Tudor and Stuart handwriting.

H. Jenkinson, *The Later Court Hands in England from the 15th to the 17th Century* (Cambridge University Press, 1927)

C. Johnson and H. Jenkinson, *English Court Hand, A.D. 1066-1500* (Cambridge University Press, 1915)

K.C. Newton, *Medieval Land Records: A Reading Aid* (Historical Association, 1971)

LATIN AND TEXT INTERPRETATION

E.A. Gooder, *Latin for Local History* (Longmans, 1978)

R.E. Latham (ed.), *Revised Medieval Latin Word List* (Oxford University Press, 1983)

C.T. Martin, *The Record Interpreter* (reprinted Phillimore & Co., 1982)

Denis Stuart, *Latin for Local and Family Historians* (Phillimore & Co., 1995). Includes a chapter on translating deed texts.

DATING

C.R. Cheney, *Handbook of Dates for Students of English History* (Cambridge University Press, 2000)

MANORIAL RECORDS

Mary Ellis, *Using Manorial Records* (Public Record Office, 1994)

P.D.A. Harvey, *Manorial Records* (British Records Association, 1984)

Patrick Palgrave-Moore, *How to Locate and Use Manorial Records* (Elvery Dowers, 1985)

Peter B. Park, *My Ancestors were Manorial Tenants* (Society of Genealogists, 1994)

Denis Stuart, *Manorial Records: an Introduction to their Transcription and Translation* (Phillimore, 1992). Little information on copyhold.

BACKGROUND AND APPLICATIONS

M.T. Clanchy, *From the Memory to Written Record* (2nd ed. Blackwell, 1993)

C. Clay, 'Landlords and Estate Management', in J. Thirsk (ed.), *The Agrarian History of England and Wales: vol.5, 1640-1750* (Cambridge University Press, 1985) vol.II, pp.119-251

B. English and John Saville, *Strict Settlement: A Guide for Historians* (University of Hull, 1983)

P.D.A. Harvey and A. McGuinness, *A Guide to British Medieval Seals* (British Library and Public Record Office, 1996)

W.G. Hoskins, *The Midland Peasant* (Leicester University Press, 1965)

H. Jenkinson, *Guide to Seals in the Public Record Office* (H.M.S.O., 1968)

D. Keene, 'The Medieval Urban Environment in Documentary Records', *Archives*, vol.16 (1983), p.137

D.H. Williams, *Welsh History Through Seals* (National Museum of Wales, 1982)

RECORD OFFICES AND COLLECTIONS

Royal Commission on Historical Manuscripts, *Record Repositories in Great Britain* (Public Record Office, 1999)

J. Foster and J. Sheppard, *British Archives* (Macmillan, 1982 and later editions)

Guide to the Public Record Office (H.M.S.O., 1963); also *Current Guide to the Contents of the Public Record Office* (H.M.S.O., 1992); see also *Records Information Leaflet 48: Private Conveyances in the Public Record Office* (1996).

Folger Shakespeare Library: *Catalogue of Manuscripts* (G.K. Hall (Boston), 1971)

Guide to British Historical Manuscripts in the Huntington Library (Huntington Library, San Marino, 1982)

The National Register of Archives and the Royal Commission on Historical Manuscripts are at Quality Court, Chancery Lane, London WC2A 1HP

The Society of Genealogists is at 14 Charterhouse Buildings, Goswell Road, London EC1M 7BA

The principal national record offices are:
Public Record Office, Ruskin Avenue, Kew, Richmond, Surrey TW9 4DU
British Library, Department of Manuscripts, 96 Euston Road, London NW1 2DB
National Library of Wales, Aberystwyth, Dyfed SY23 3BY
University Library, West Road, Cambridge CB3 9DR
Bodleian Library, Oxford OX1 3BG

WEB SITES

Warning: These are correct at the time of writing, but Web addresses frequently change and, if they fail to work, you may need to search for the site.

National Register of Archives:
http://www.hmc.gov.uk/main.htm (includes a link to the partly computerised Manorial Register)
For ARCHON (listing of Record Offices including web sites where they exist): http://www.hmc.gov.uk/archon/archon.htm
For NRA Reports: http://www.hmc.gov.uk/nra/nra2.htm

Public Record Office:
http://www.pro.gov.uk/ (includes a link to the A2A [Access to Archives] lists)
On-line catalogue: http://catalogue.pro.gov.uk/ListInt/Default.asp

British Library Manuscript Catalogue:
http://molcat.bl.uk/

Essex Record Office:
http://www.essexcc.gov.uk/heritage/ero/seax/default.htm

Surrey History Centre:
http://shs.surreycc.gov.uk

Gwynedd Archives Service:
http://www.gwynedd.gov.uk/archives

University of Hull Library:
http://www.hull.ac.uk/lib/archives/contents.html

University of Nottingham:
http://mss.library.nottingham.ac.uk

Harvard University Law Library:
http://www.law.harvard.edu/library/special/collections/manuscripts/deeds/index.htm

GLOSSARY OF DEED TERMS

Abstract of Title: summary of prior ownership, prepared when a property was about to be sold.

Abuttal: names of owners or tenants of property adjoining that involved in a deed, recorded as an aid to identification.

Assignment: transfer of a right, usually a lease, or a mortgage; **assignment to attend the inheritance**: assignment of the residue of a mortgage term to a trustee, after the mortgage has been paid off.

Attorney: see **Letter of Attorney**

Bargain and Sale: deed (usually 16th-century) transferring property, rendered valid by **Enrolment**.

Bond (also **Recognisance**): agreement to pay a financial penalty if specified conditions are not met. A **Recognisance in the nature of a Statute Staple** was a strong form of bond that was normally cancelled by a separate deed, a **Defeasance**.

Burgage Tenure: type of tenure in a borough, similar in its rights to **Freehold**, often involving the payment of a uniform burgage rent for each plot.

Cartulary: volume containing copies of deeds (often with other material), most often compiled by a monastery.

Consideration: the purchase money for a property.

Copy of Court Roll: copy of entry on roll of manor court proceedings, recording admission of a tenant to his holding, and serving as a title deed. See **Copyhold**.

Copyhold: property held by copy of court roll.

Counterpart: the second half of an indenture, precisely matching the first part; usually used for the second copy of a lease, signed by the tenant and retained by the grantor.

Covenant: an agreement entered into by one of the parties to a deed; a **covenant for production of title deeds** is an agreement to produce deeds not being handed over to a purchaser.

Curtilage: yard or court associated with a dwelling house.

Defeasance: see **Bond**

Dower: the right of a widow to a third of her late husband's property; a dower trustee might hold it on his behalf to prevent a claim for dower.

Endorsement: the writing on the back (dorse) of a deed.

Enrolment: the copy of a deed on a roll kept by a court as a permanent record.

Entail: the settlement of property so that it must descend to the owner's heirs in a specified fashion, and not be sold or otherwise dispersed. The current owner of entailed property is then a **tenant for life** and his next heir is the **tenant in tail**.

Equity of Redemption: the right of a mortgagor to redeem the property he has mortgaged, even if the due time for repayment has passed; this right could be granted to someone else.

Executor: the person appointed to carry out the provisions of a will.

Exemplification: Formal copy of a court record issued with the court's seal. The most common exemplifications are those of **Recoveries** (q.v.) but **Exemplifications of Fines** are sometimes found, as are exemplifications of Chancery decrees or proceedings.

Fee-farm: see **Rent**

Feoffee see **Trustee**

Feoffment: a simple grant of property.

Fine: (a) Entry Fine: sum of money paid for the granting of a lease or for admission to a copyhold tenement; (b) Final Concord: record of collusive court case in the Court of Common Pleas, provided as two matching copies (Left and Right-hand Indentures of Fine); the Foot of Fine is the third copy of the record, kept by the Court; **Deed to Lead the Uses of a Fine**: agreement to levy a fine, and to declare the uses for which the property is held.

Freehold: tenure **in fee simple**, i.e. absolute and unlimited, though possibly paying a fixed rent (a chief rent or fee-farm rent).

Gift: any transfer of real property in the medieval period is described as a gift, in contrast to a grant of rights, tithes, etc.

Grant: see **Gift**, **Reversion**

Heriot: a fine paid on the death of a tenant (holding by copy or by three-life lease), either a sum of money (often a year's chief rent) or the best beast or best possession). For a freeholder, the similar payment was known as a **Relief** (q.v.).

Indenture: deeds with the top indented, in principle prepared in two or more identical copies, one for each party; see **Counterpart**.

Knight Service: the feudal tenure of a manor, by providing the service of a knight or part of one (or in the post-medieval period, by a payment in lieu of this).

Lease: grant of property to a tenant for a specified period, usually a term of years; types of lease include **life lease**: lease for the life of the tenant; **three-life lease**: lease until the deaths have occurred of three named people (with an upper limit of 99 years); **'perpetual' lease**: intended to continue indefinitely, granted for a very long period, e.g. 1,000 years; **building lease**: lease, generally for 99 years, including an agreement for the tenant to build a house. See **Reversion**; **Counterpart**.

Leasehold: tenure by lease.

Lease and Release: post-medieval transfer of property by granting a lease for a year (sometimes six months), and then releasing the grantor's rights the following day.

Letter of Attorney: deed establishing a substitute to act for one of the parties in a transaction (in the medieval period, usually to grant or receive Seizin).

Letter Patent: royal grant, enrolled on the Patent Rolls.

Licence to Alienate: royal permission, by Letters Patent, to sell or dispose of a property obtained from the Crown and held by knight service.

Messuage: standard term for a property including a dwelling house.

Moiety: half of a property, often **undivided moiety**, when the shares of the two owners have not been separated or physically divided.

Partition: division of a property between two or more interested parties.

Precipe: see **Recovery**

Probate: the establishment of the validity of a will in a church court, recorded in the **grant of probate**.

Quitclaim: deed renouncing any possible right to a property.

Recital: rehearsal of prior event and deeds affecting a property being transferred.

Recognisance: see **Bond**

Recovery: collusive law suit in the Court of Common Pleas, normally used to destroy (bar) or alter an entail; its result are recorded in an **Exemplification** of a (Common) Recovery; **a Deed to make a tenant to the Precipe** precedes a Recovery, transferring the property involved to a trustee and declaring the uses for which it is held.

Regnal Year: the current year of a king's reign, counting from his accession, used as the means of dating deeds until the mid-17th century.

Release: see **Lease and Release**

Relief: manorial payment from a freeholding required for the heir to inherit or for the property to be sold.

Rent: payment due for use of property; **chief rent** or **quit rent**; a fixed rent due from a freehold property; a **fee-farm** or **reserved rent** is similar, set up on the sale of property by a grant in fee farm.

Reversion: The return of leased property to the original owner on expiry of a lease. A **Grant** (or **Lease**) **in reversion** started after the termination of a previous lease, or sometimes after some other specified time or event.

Seizin: the possession of freehold property; **livery of seizin** is the ceremony of taking possession by physical transfer of a turf, key, etc.

Settlement: transfer of property to trustees, for a particular purpose; **marriage settlement**: settlement preceding (**pre-nuptial**) or occasionally following a marriage (**post-nuptial**), involving property held for the benefit of husband, wife and children; **family settlement**: settlement of property to descend to the owner's heir(s) and other children, i.e. establishing an **entail**.

Statute Staple: see **Bond**

Surrender: the return of property held by lease or by copyhold to the lessor or the lord of the manor.

Tenant for Life and **Tenant in tail**: see **Entail**

Tenement: a formal description of any type of property, but particularly property including a building.

Tenure: the form of right by which property is held. See also **Burgage tenure**; **Copyhold**; **Freehold**; **Knight Service**; **Leasehold**.

Trustee: person holding property on behalf of another, for specified uses. See also
 Dower. A **feoffee** holds property similarly, but without specification of the uses.

Uses: the purposes for which property is held by a trustee, in a marriage or family
 Settlement, etc.

Virgate: see **Yardland**

Warranty: an undertaking by a grantor to support a new owner's title to a
 property.

Yardland or **Virgate**: an area of land (usually in common fields), conventionally
 of 32 acres, but in reality varying very much from place to place; holdings were
 often described by the number of yardlands they contained.

INDEX OF SUBJECTS

INDEX OF PERSONS AND PLACES